Fait

John Selwyn Gummer is Minister of State, Ministry of Agriculture, Fisheries and Food. He has written and contributed to several books, including *The Permissive Society* (1971) and *The Christian Calendar* (1974).

Eric Heffer, a former Minister of State for Trade and Industry, was a member of the Labour Party National Executive Committee from 1975–86. He is the author of *Labour's Future: Socialist or SDP Mark II?*(1986).

Alan Beith is the Deputy Leader of the Parliamentary Liberal Party and Alliance Spokesman on Foreign and Commonwealth Affairs. He is the author of *The Case for the Liberal Party and the Alliance* (1983).

Faith in Politics

Which Way Should Christians Vote?

JOHN SELWYN GUMMER

ERIC HEFFER

ALAN BEITH

First published in Great Britain 1987 by
SPCK, Holy Trinity Church, Marylebone Road, London, NW1 4DU

British Library Cataloguing in Publication Data

Gummer, John Selwyn
    Faith in politics: which way should
    Christians vote?
    1. Political parties——Religious aspects
    ——Christianity   2. Political parties——
    Great Britain
    I. Title   II. Heffer, Eric   III. Beith, Alan
    261.7   BR115.P7

    ISBN 0–281–04299–3

    Photoset by Deltatype, Ellesmere Port
    Printed in Great Britain by
    Hazell Watson & Viney Ltd
    Member of the BPCC group
    Aylesbury, Bucks

Contents

Part One

The Case for the Conservatives

JOHN SELWYN GUMMER

Christianity is in the business of politics

If we believe that God can be bothered about human beings at all, then the miracles of the Virgin Birth and the resurrection are not difficult to accept. 'Every hair of your head is numbered' is far harder to believe than the Empty Tomb. The idea that the Almighty Creator cares about me (and, perhaps more surprisingly, my neighbour) is one which utterly transforms our view of the world.

It is an awe-inspiring claim. It means that faith cannot be excluded from any part of life. The intense involvement of God in human affairs as Creator, Saviour and Sustainer makes Christianity, in William Temple's words, 'the most materialist of religions'.

The incarnation is witness to God's full-hearted commitment to the whole of human life. Therefore anyone who asserts that the Church ought not to be involved in politics is denying the central fact of the Christian faith. True God and true man means exactly that; the Creator has immersed himself in his creation and identified himself even with the mess that man has made of it. That is why the Christ of the carpenter's shop cannot be excluded from decisions about social security any more than Jesus the Jew can be left out of a consideration of race.

The Church cannot help meddling in politics just as, despite Lord Melbourne's assertion, it cannot help meddling in people's private lives. Indeed, where politicians take a greater role in society, so the Church's political involvement will increase. The more people look to the state to solve their problems, the more the Church will need to concern itself with the decisions of government and the agenda of political parties.

By what authority?

Yet the terms upon which the Church intervenes are of crucial importance. It is essential that we make a clear difference between the distinctive Christian input on the one hand, and any party-political views that spokesmen for the Church may have, on the other. It needs always to be abundantly clear that a pronouncement comes from the gospel and not from a party-political stance dressed up as Christianity.

A single example will suffice. Politicians have been concerned at the decline in rural transport and have sought ways of improving the opportunities for those in the country who have no access to cars. As a Conservative Government sought to bring more operators and greater competition into the routes, so the argument has crystallized into one about deregulation. The Church has, obviously, a contribution to make to the discussion. It is a voice for those who might otherwise be forgotten and it does have a good deal of understanding about rural life with its network of country parishes and village churches. It would therefore be perfectly proper for a bishop to remind the government of its responsibilities to the poor and to see that the demands of the gospel had an impact upon the decisions which were being made.

Yet the Bishop of Durham went much further. He suggested that deregulation itself was not a policy which Christians could support. Now that proposition is clearly not defensible as an episcopal utterance, although it might be thought a suitably controversial view for Professor Jenkins! What was dangerous about the pronouncement was that it destroyed any likelihood of Transport Ministers listening to him seriously, and an opportunity for Christian witness was lost. It is difficult enough for the Church to be heard, without erecting unnecessary barriers.

In fact, of course, we are back again with the pope and Galileo. The pope was wrong to tell Galileo that he must obey in matters of physics. He was mistaken in claiming that

4

the Church had a Christian insight which could overrule scientific fact. He confused the need of Christians to uphold the centrality of God's creation with his desire to assert the physical centrality of the earth in the universe. We have learned better since, but the Church still suffers from the damage done. Pronouncing on party-political issues carries the same danger. Therefore deregulation is not an issue upon which the Church can properly have a view. Indeed, to claim one makes it less likely that the Church will be listened to when it does have a right to speak.

Christian politicians must not be let off the hook. They need constantly to be reminded of the priorities which the gospel imposes. They should never be given an excuse to forget the imperatives which faith demands. They must therefore never be allowed to write off the Church's comments as politically motivated. Bishops must beware of the temptation to seek to seem relevant by second-guessing politicians and doing the work which they ought to be doing. Perhaps there is some hint of the temptation of our Lord looking down from the high mountain upon the nations of the earth. Instead the Church must seek to influence the agenda and the priorities, because Christians can agree on ends even where it is wholly permissible for them to disagree on means.

This distinction is of course a difficult one to draw. Passionate belief in a particular political stance makes it hard not to blur the distinction between political views and gospel demands. Faith infuses the whole of a Christian's life. His habit of thought is moulded by his habit of worship, prayer and belief. The springs of his personality are fed by the teachings of the Church and the witness of Scripture. He cannot separate what he thinks, from what he believes and what he is.

Yet the attempt to distinguish between political views and religious truth must be made. Otherwise, we shall claim for our mundane partialities a divine authority which ought not to dignify them. In doing so, we shall detract from the magisterial demands which faith properly makes upon Christian politicians.

That has all too often been the case when a particular political party has taken the name 'Christian'. It is not surprising that, in the battle to rebuild Europe after the Second World War, men such as Konrad Adenauer and Alcide de Gasperi created Christian Democrat parties to draw upon the strength of the Christian faith. They rightly saw Christianity as a bulwark against oppression and a guarantee of civilized values. Yet they also assumed a Christian consensus in political action which is not borne out by the facts. There is no way in which the gospels can be said to lay down a blueprint for action by government in a modern state. In practical terms we have seen that Christian Democrat parties have been unable to agree among themselves as to a joint economic programme. However they may wish it were not so, they are centre and centre-right parties opposed by Liberals and socialists. They have a clear place in the political spectrum and it is one which is not occupied by all Christians. For that reason they cannot suggest that a Christian can only vote for the Christian party. Nor can they say that every socialist in Germany or Italy is an atheist!

In Britain, with no tradition of confessional parties outside the Irish question, there are still some who maintain a kind of Christian exclusivity for the party of their choice. For example, Lord Soper clearly finds it almost impossible to believe that a Christian can be anything other than a socialist. His political stance and his party allegiance are part and parcel of his view of the gospel. Christians who are not socialists need to answer this position, which is frequently taken, not only by the articulate Lord Soper, but by many others. Indeed, there are those who are not socialists themselves but who assume that Christ preached a primitive sort of socialism which Christians would support if only it did not seem so impractical. And there is of course the strong tradition of Christian socialism in Britain and the even more widespread attitude of clergymen who speak and act as if left-wing programmes are inevitably more Christian than others. Their identification of Christianity with the policies of the left needs to be challenged, and the current debate about South Africa will serve as an example.

Christian duties or political policies?
Christians believe in the Fatherhood of God and therefore in the brotherhood of man. A political system which treats some of God's children as inherently inferior to others because of the colour of their skins, cannot be supported by Christians. It is therefore right to oppose apartheid on religious grounds and for the Church to provide a voice for the oppressed peoples. The problem comes when Christians, properly involved in the struggle, begin to suggest that some ways of ending the system are more Christian than others. These proponents of economic sanctions and disinvestment claim them as Christians duties rather than political policies.

Archbishop Tutu has certainly put the case in this way. We must of course listen to him carefully. When he speaks of the evil of racism he speaks for the Church. Yet it is just not true that his views on disinvestment are inherently more Christian than those of Chief Buthelesi and it is wholly wrong to unchurch the one because of the stand of the other. The issue between them is not a moral one but a matter of political judgement.

And it is a judgement which can divide Christians in all countries. There is room for a real debate as to whether disinvestment and economic sanctions will bring about reconciliation. Christians can properly disagree about the charity involved in destroying jobs in order to force the collapse of apartheid, and they can wonder whether such a collapse would have the results for which we all pray. There are no particular methods to further harmony in South Africa laid down for us in the Gospels or taught by the Church. Our policies come from human attempts to put into practice gospel principles. In trying to see the mind of Christ we must use our reason to choose what seems the most effective way of achieving his ends. That is why Christian politicians and church spokesmen must be so careful lest they clothe their political views in the cope of religious truth and ascribe to Christ the product of their human judgements.

We must start from the assumption that there is room for Christians to disagree about means even when there is a clear identity of ends. Just as there is no justification in claiming a specifically Christian political solution to the problems of South Africa, so there is no way in which we ought to propose that Christians must be wedded to a particular political programme. Indeed, in arguing that a Christian does not have to be a socialist, we have to be very careful not to fall into the trap of arguing that he *does* have to be a Conservative. That would be no more proper a view than Lord Soper's. The most that one ought to claim for a political party is that its analysis of the human condition is closest to one's understanding of the Christian faith. It is my contention that Conservative policies derive from a view of how God's world works, which is nearest to what I discern the Gospels to proclaim.

Christian choice and Christian freedom

We being where Julian of Norwich begins in her *Revelations of Divine Love*. It is with the glorious belief that 'God made us, God loveth us and God keepeth us'. It is that assertion of individual worth which closes off a number of political options and dictates some political priorities. You cannot be a racist and a Christian; nor a Fascist, nor a Marxist. All three are philosophies which inherently rely on the notion of valuing the individual not as a child of God but as a member of a group. His or her worth depends on race, class or party.

8

By their tokens, the man who fell among thieves would be the Samaritan's neighbour only if his colour, his social position or his political record fitted.

Yet if this belief closes off options, it also creates presumptions. God chose no corporate salvation but called men individually. He refused to compel men and women to be good but sought instead to win them to him: the Creator wooing his creatures! Indeed, in order that we may love him he gave us the opportunity to hate him. That is the choice between heaven and hell. Choice lies at the heart of the Christian revelation. For love cannot compel. It cannot be love unless it is free love. The person who cannot choose to hate, cannot love. God allowed us to choose hell in order that we might have the chance to choose heaven. Travelling the narrow way presupposes the possibility of treading the broad road that leads to perdition.

It would be odd then, would it not, if God were to give his creatures choice in what matters most, only to insist that man should take away choice in what matters much less? There is something wrong in believing a man fit to choose his eternal destiny but not to decide on the education of his children.

Politicians are inclined to believe that choice in anything really worthwhile is a dangerous thing for ordinary mortals. That belief usually carries the unspoken addendum that politicians are of course themselves fully capable of exercising choice not only for themselves but for others. It is the argument of the tyrant down the ages and it should be suspect even when presented by democratic socialists. Local councillors whose opposition to single-sex schools or denominational education leads them to suggest that parents do not know enough about education to make these choices for their children; shadow ministers who are so committed to the Comprehensive principle that they will not accept local option; Parties so sure that they are right about independent education as a bar to their egalitarianism, that they demand its abolition. All these have to answer the fundamental question – by what right do you take away choice from human beings whom God distinguishes from all his creation by the ability to choose?

Politicians of the left are tempted to reply that because not everybody has a chance to choose, then the privileges of those who can choose must be taken away. The commitment to human equality outweighs the demands of divine choice. Indeed, it is often suggested that there really is something immoral in choice because it is bound to be unfairly distributed and its exercise has a tendency to increase inequality.

This proposition has to be faced by Christians in any case and in a fundamental and acute way. We have to reconcile our belief in the uniqueness of the revelation of Christ with the undoubted fact that information about it is vouchsafed most unequally. Many die in ignorance of him, many more have him presented so inadequately or in so deformed a way that they cannot reasonably accept him. The opportunity to choose Christ is not open to all. In the most important matter there can be, people are manifestly unequal. Our response to that fact is the missionary endeavour. Even though we cannot reach all, we must spread the gospel to as many as we can. That which is so important ought not to remain the privilege of the few, but must be preached to all nations that they may have the chance to choose. Our fundamental Christian attitude, enjoined upon us in the Gospels, is to spread the privilege of choice to the many instead of abolishing it for the few.

Now that is surely the spirit behind Conservative policy. It is to spread to the many the privileges once restricted to the few. No privilege is more important than that which most distinguishes humanity – the privilege of choice. Tory concern with choice explains why every major reform of education has been Conservative-inspired. Free primary education for all, secondary education available to all, higher education open to all – these were measures which arose from the Tory preoccupation with education, not least as the provider and informer of wider choice.

So too it has been with housing. Back in 1951 when the Labour Party lost power, Britain had only 18 per cent of its homes owned by their occupiers. By 1986, thirty-five years later, the figure was 62 per cent of a very much larger total. Millions more had a real stake in their future and a real independence from tenancy. This change has been achieved partly by the sale of council houses but much more by the tax encouragement given to home ownership.

The debate on this issue is an instructive one for Christians because it throws up very clearly the issue between choice and equality. Those who saw tenancy as the norm in the 1950s suggested that the home owner had a privilege which it would be better to restrict in the name of equality. They pointed to the 80 per cent and asked why the few should have what the many did not. The incoming Tory Government took the opposite view. They sought to extend the idea of ownership and choice to the many. It has taken thirty years to achieve this reversal and there is still more to do, even though there will obviously always be some who through choice or necessity will rent rather than buy.

It is, however, certainly true that the property-owning democracy involves a degree of inequality which an all-tenant society does not have. It also involves a degree of freedom which an all-tenant society can never manage. It does seem much more in accordance with the Christian view of human nature that we should prefer freedom to equality. After all, in all the things that we would say really mattered, we do just that. For centuries men have fought to be free to think and worship as they wish. It is only in a period when we have elevated the material above all else, that we can seriously put forward the proposition that men and women should be free in all things spiritual but confined in things material. To the medieval mind this would have been absolutely incomprehensible. A man is what he believes. To protect him from false doctrine was an obvious duty – to protect him from business failure was unthought of. We have reversed the hierarchy of values but we still often retain the medieval belief in compulsion. We do not lay much store by people's personal beliefs, so we feel free to leave them alone. However, we think their material well-being so important that we are prepared to restrict their freedom in order that they may conform to our view of a proper ordering of a materialist society.

Freedoms of the economy and of the spirit

That is the contention of the democratic socialist. The real distinction between him and his communist fellows is that he clings to the liberal values in cultural matters while denying them in economic affairs. His passion for equality leads him to seek to iron out material differences while protesting a special interest in protecting freedom of the spirit. For the Christian this dualism is impossible.

First, there is no proper theological base for making so sharp a division. The doctrine of the resurrection of the body affirms our commitment to the view that we cannot separate the spiritual and the material. The concept of a Creator and incarnate God binds spiritual and material indissolubly. If we think that freedom of thought and speech, of worship and belief is vital for the flowering of mankind, then we have no theological base for excluding freedom in things material. It is only if we think there is something unworthy in the physical and material that we can sustain that division. We have to embrace the heretical views of the Albigensians – and even I would not like to accuse the Bishop of Liverpool of that!

But of course the reason that socialists make this distinction is their higher valuation of things material. They do think that the material is more important than the spiritual. Their Marxism lays such stress upon the importance of economic factors and the class struggle that they are bound instinctively to believe that the vital thing is to establish economic equality, as that is the determining factor in society. That evaluation poses a real problem to the

Christian. If I am to allow a man the right to choose for himself in matters which concern his eternal soul, then who am I to restrict his choice in matters which concern only his material well-being?

At this point most take refuge in a pragmatic argument. Freedom of thought and speech, they say, can be protected even if there is no freedom of economic activity. Further, one person's freedom to create capital, to spend and to own is bought at the cost of others. Yet neither of these propositions can really be defended. There cannot be freedom of thought or of speech if there is no dispersal of capital. If the state owns all the means of spreading ideas, proving theories, researching theses and developing products, then how can freedom be protected? The recent accident at Chernobyl provides an example. If there is only one employer of scientists, then who will quarrel with the official assurance that a particular nuclear design is safe? If only one agency owns all the media, then where will the dissident make his challenge to the scientific establishment? If the entire production of nuclear hardware is in the hands of one organization, then where will the unrecognized inventor get support for his prototype or his modification? It is only by the diffusion and the independence of capital that we are able to protect the freedom of speech and thought which as Christians we believe is essential for a person to be truly human.

And the proof of the theory is in the reality. It is a fact that no major discovery of life-saving drugs has been achieved in the Soviet Union since the War. Almost every medical advance has come from the free countries, where drug companies have funded their own research, driven on by private profit and kept open to new ideas by competition. It is indeed capitalism which has ensured the real freedom of ideas and not socialism.

But, say the democratic socialists, that is all in a totalitarian society. We want the equality of socialism without the manifest lack of freedom one sees in Russia. That way we can ensure that the poor are not exploited while still protecting the right of free men and women to think and say what they will. Sadly, the evidence is wholly against this comfortable theory. A quick look at the arguments of democratic socialist councillors in Ealing or Brent and we see the inevitability of their opposition to freedom. Children must be taught that heterosexism is wrong and that homosexual practice is of equal worth to heterosexual love. That is necessary because otherwise there would not be equality between the two groups. Racial equality is of such importance that teachers who draw any distinction on any grounds must be persecuted. Ray Honeyford may not even demand a change in policy on behalf of his Asian pupils without being booted out on grounds of racism. Of course, some of the more lunatic views expressed must not be taken as typical of socialism as a whole. Yet many of these extreme attitudes are the inevitable result of the socialist's basic belief in equality. If you think that equality is the most important thing in a society then you will be prepared to take very tough action to ensure that it can be established.

Indeed, you will take the democratic socialist view that all children should be educated in one system whether the parents like it or not. You will be prepared, as is the British Labour Party, to abolish private education on the basis that it allows a choice which increases inequality. You will therefore remove the freedom of the few in order to further the equality of the many. That is a procedure which seems wholly contrary to God's dealing with man. The Creator freed his creature even to the extent of allowing him to choose his own destruction. There is little basis for human egalitarianism there! I have therefore to prefer the optimistic view of the Conservative who seeks to spread choice and reduce unfairness by ever wider opportunity. It is the only way to free the human spirit. Where the search for equality dominates the political system, there the human spirit is caged.

Freedom to help the poor

The Christian Conservative cannot leave the argument there. He naturally insists that socialism is not nearer the mind of Christ than free-enterprise capitalism. He points to the need to spread freedom of choice and demands that economic freedom is an essential prerequisite of all freedom. What he then has to face up to is the problem of poverty. Christians have a special concern for the poor and a real worry about the dangers of riches. How then does a Conservative deal with the assertion that his insistence upon freedom condemns the poor to their poverty and ensures that the privileged are bound to come off best?

It is an argument which we are always hearing asserted as if self-evident. Tax-cuts throughout the scale are seen as specially helpful to the rich, simply because the better-off pay more tax and therefore a one-per-cent reduction has a greater impact on a large income. The gap between rich and poor is felt to increase even though the low-wage earner actually has more to spend. General rises in the standard of living mean an increase in society's view of the minimum level of life. Therefore the poor remain with us, as poverty is redefined by reference to riches. If the lowest quartile is the definition of poverty, then poverty can never be eradicated, because there is always a lowest quartile!

Today it is claimed that a family is poor if it cannot afford a colour television set, a night out, a holiday, or a washing machine. All these are advantages which were once the exclusive property of the rich. The fact that there are those who cannot afford them is often blamed by those on the left upon inequalities in society. In fact it is those very inequalities which have made it possible for the poor ever to dream of these advantages. It is precisely because the rich have been in a privileged position at an earlier stage that these opportunities have become available and, in a market economy, have increasingly been spread. In Britain today the rich are getting richer and so are the poor. That is true in two different senses. There is the absolute sense that those on social security are in receipt of benefits which are now worth more in real terms than was the case in 1979. It is also true in the relative sense that we demand for the poor a much higher minimum standard than was conceivable a very short time ago. In this country the goal-posts are constantly being moved as we insist that the decent level increases as society's expectations increase.

But how do those expectations increase? That is a vital question if we think that a bath and an indoor loo are worthwhile improvements – let alone television sets and holidays. They increase because there are those in our society with the extra purchasing power to make them increase: people who pioneer the improvement of living standards simply by having the financial ability to make wider choices. What they choose they popularize and the market – an essentially democratic mechanism – spreads more widely. In a free society, the poor get richer not in spite of the rich but because of them. Anyone who produces an improvement taken up by the well-off has a vested interest in spreading the opportunity to buy to others who are less well-off. There is a natural tendency in capitalism to encourage the spread of wealth in order to increase markets and opportunities for wealth creation. No wonder that the business community in South Africa is acknowledged to be among the most enlightened sections of white society. They have a vested interest in bigger markets and in a population which is better educated, fed and housed. Capitalism has a natural tendency to increase the capital of skills and other human stock as well as the accumulation and dispersal of money.

Yet there is no inevitability about the poor getting richer. It is so much a fact of life in our free society that we tend to take it for granted. In closed societies improvements in the standards of the population are by no means inevitable. Take the recent history of Czechoslovakia as an example. Before the War it would have been numbered among the developed societies with a fairly sophisticated industrial base in some regions and a spread of wealth and living standards reasonably comparable with its neighbours to the west. Now, after many years of the enforcement of equality, it is relatively much poorer than it was, very much less innovative, and impoverished culturally as well as industrially.

The Christian ought, then, to face up to that economic fact that it is capitalism which has created the wealth of nations and not socialism. Yet we rightly fear unbridled capitalism. If the market forces are allowed to reign supreme with no restriction then there are prices which Christians would not be prepared to pay. There is a natural tendency towards monopoly. Men like to corner the market as it makes their lives so much easier! Yet monopoly destroys choice and works against the interests of the consumer. Monopolies do not tend towards the creation and dispersal of wealth but rather to its comfortable retention in the hands of those who control the monopoly.

We have seen that at work in Britain during the run-up to the privatization of British Telecom. The old view was that you could have any colour of telephone as long as it was black and you did not mind waiting. You could have a telephone answering-machine as long as the Post Office put it in and you rented it at a high price. A firm which perfected a clip-on aid for the deaf was threatened with prosecution because the Post Office had not approved it. All was extremely cosy – for those in authority in management and unions alike.

The coming of privatization and competition – even of the limited kind possible in this sort of service – changed all that. There is real choice and a wider range of services. You even get an answer when you dial 192! (Not always, but much more often.) Investment decisions are now in the hands of those who are subject to consumer and shareholder choice rather than those in government trying to balance the political demands of the Post Office and the coal industry, not to mention the political demands within the Post Office between telephones and postal services.

It is the business of government to retain the independence necessary to restrain monopoly and protect the customer. It cannot do that if it is both judge and jury. If it owns the business then it cannot protect the customer from its own decisions. Indeed there is a natural tendency of monopoly to favour the staff against the customer. That is reinforced when the monopoly is state-controlled. Actions to protect the position of the staff or to enhance their pay or continue their restrictive practices can always be paraded as compassion. Yet the cost is rarely counted: cost to the taxpayer who is less able to compete and employ as a result; cost to other industries in the state sector which are starved of necessary capital; cost to the consumer whose choice is restricted and who usually foots the bill.

The moral duty of the government is to keep itself free to intervene against the damaging effects of monopoly. It then puts itself on the side of the weak against the strong. It supports the poor against the privileged. It ensures that the voice of the unorganized is heard against the bellowing of the organized. Government is fulfilling the Christian duty of a bias towards the poor. It must do so confronted with public or private monopolies although it finds it much more difficult when its own interests are at stake. Government can demand that Tate and Lyle or Ferruzzi go before the Monopolies and Mergers Commission without much problem. It is far harder not to plead some sort of public interest when faced with the monopoly practices of British Coal. When it comes to judging what is good for the coal industry, we know only too well who the main shareholder is and who wields the strongest pressures inside the organization. Neither is primarily affected by the consumer's choice.

It is this outside intervening role which most befits government and most frees it to fight on behalf of the poor. The Christian view is surely best reflected by a determination not to leave the market to develop unimpeded but to intervene positively to maintain competition. It is that competition which is most able to ensure that capitalism is fair and it is competition which makes for the extension of choice and of wealth.

Freedom to create new jobs and industries

Yet even those Christians who would go along with this analysis find a real problem in what seems to be the unfairness shown by the North/South divide. They long to do something about the unequal distribution of profitable industry and the regional inequalities of employment opportunities. It is a real concern and it drives some to propose draconian solutions. Perhaps the most useful recent presentation of this issue is in Bishop David Sheppard's Book *Bias to the Poor*. In it he demands, for example, that the new industries settled in the Thames Valley should be directed to Liverpool whether they like it or not. Businessmen have chosen the Thames Valley as the most effective place, geographically and sociologically, for them to site their enterprise and use their talents and resources. The Bishop asks governments to second-guess their commercial judgements by directing them to move elsewhere in the UK. That credits the Government with an ability of which there is not much empirical evidence. In fact it would be bound to fail. Companies would go elsewhere in Europe rather than site themselves disadvantageously in the UK. We should thereby lose jobs and revenue for the whole of Britain and not just for Merseyside. Indeed, we could only do this if we were to renege on our commitment to the European Community to safeguard freedom of establishment. It would seem also to conflict with the Christian duty to seek to allow men and women to make their own decisions with the talents at their disposal.

The problem with the proposal is that it betrays a refusal to think through what is superficially an attractive concept. It also comes oddly in a book where, in other sections, the

Bishop defends the Church's closure of redundant churches as proper stewardship of its resources. It would seem reasonable then for businessmen too to have the duty to close factories which are no longer profitable in order to strengthen businesses producing goods and services that people want. Yet even with its obvious flaws, there is a real attraction in a policy which seeks radically to ensure that the benefits of growth and expansion are not restricted to the South but are spread north of the Trent. We can share that feeling of unfairness but we must beware of investing it with an absolute moral authority. There is no gospel demand for geographically equal economic development. Were there such an imperative, then the Bishop of Liverpool would have to insist that industry should be directed from the Thames Valley, not to Merseyside, but to Burundi or the Southern Sudan!

Nor is it so easy a practical choice. In insisting that the Rootes Group should plan its development away from the West Midlands the government of the day contributed to the company's demise and Birmingham's decline. The practical problem is therefore that a government's attempt to site industrial development away from the place that is commercially indicated, may be very well motivated but is often disastrous. In attempting a fairer distribution of jobs and wealth, it often ensures a real loss of both.

An historical example will serve to emphasize the point. If a government had sought to keep the wool-manufacturing centres of Norfolk and Suffolk alive and this had become an accustomed part of political policy, then Bradford may never have had its chance. That would have been Britain's loss, for the advantages which made us the centre of a great world manufacturing business may well not have obtained were the wool industry centred in East Anglia. So, just as the Church of England ought not now to keep up the wool churches at the expense of preaching the gospel in Milton Keynes, so governments cannot seek to maintain or direct industry in more difficult areas when that destroys our ability to effect growth in more favoured locations.

The direction myth persists even to a ridiculous degree as any who have read the Second Reading debate of the Felixstowe Dock Bill will recognize. There, Members of Parliament were objecting to the extension of Felixstowe on the basis that there was plenty of space for ships to land goods in ports on the other side of the country. The fact that the boats would choose to go to Rotterdam rather than Liverpool still seems remote to them. Indeed, the whole of the Labour Party programme for the docks industry in the 1983 General Election was based upon the government direction of ships to the port which the government thought most suitable for social rather than commercial reasons.

Again we can sympathize with the attitude behind the policy. It does seem hard to accept that geographical and industrial facts are so difficult to control. Man wants to feel he is master of his destiny and Christian man is inclined to think it is almost idolatrous if we accept that there are certain underlying rules which we break at our peril. Somehow it does not seem very compassionate to insist that Liverpool's geographical position which was the reason for its growth when Britain traded by sea with the Americas is now the reason for its decline as our trading patterns have changed towards the rest of Europe. Yet all that reasonable believers in the market are saying is that the world works in certain ways and that governments have only limited scope to affect those basic market laws. It is hardly compassionate to ignore those facts when to do so puts off the hour when reality asserts itself in what is often a much more devastating manner. Christian unreality can do just as much damage as anyone else's.

The truth is that we are not going to be successful in avoiding permanently the operation of the market but that does not mean that there is nothing that we can do to improve the prospects of an unloved region. It is, for example, perfectly possible to try to make up for the temporary difficulties which might overwhelm an industry or a region which otherwise would be unable to weather the storm. Direct government help to cushion industry from the effects of unfair competition, sudden disaster, or the provision of help for restructuring or re-equipment must be sensible steps. We need always to be on our guard, however, lest we allow our hearts to rule our heads. The trouble with the heart is that it has to have an immediate response. We feel a need and we allow ourselves to be bounced into short-term solutions which may in the longer term make things a good deal worse. Too lax a regional policy can easily mean that we shall be open to the danger of taxing successful companies so that they become uncompetitive while spending money on failing companies which have no hope of ever competing. At all points we have the real problem of the Government seeking to make commercial judgements with which it has never shown itself much at home.

Of course, there are many ways in which the improvement of infrastructure – the building of roads and the provision of airlinks – can make regions more accessible. This can be a crucial factor where geographical disadvantage has been the block. So too, much can be done by presentation where there is a major psychological problem which afflicts businessmen who might otherwise choose to locate their companies in less favoured areas. There is no doubt that the long-standing reputation that Liverpool has had for bad labour relations has been a bar to its resurgence. The work of the Bishop and Archbishop, among others, has been valuable in painting a better and more accurate picture. Even where there is no such overriding image to be countered there is often a real need to ensure that decisions for location are made on real commercial grounds and not upon inherited dislikes and personal convenience. Anyone who has relocated a business outside London will know how difficult it is to convince senior management that there is life outside the South East!

There is much which specialized training and improved

education can do to make less favoured areas of the country more likely to attract new jobs. Areas which for a long time have had an economy based upon heavy industry with very little experience of small business or self-employment present particular problems which can only be overcome by a real effort at retraining and the provision of special help for those willing to try to set up on their own. There is often a shortage of the kind of skills which are taken for granted in the South. Secretarial recruitment, for example, can be a major problem in an area where the educational system has not been used to teach the office skills or even, in some cases, basic spelling and composition.

Nor is it unreasonable to provide temporary encouragement for business to use to overcome the initial difficulties of relocation or the problems of moving from an area where they may well have started entirely fortuitously. It is not a credible view that every business decision has been made on strictly commercial or logical grounds! Nonetheless we do no one any good by so skewing the advantages to locate in a wholly unsatisfactory place that we weaken a business, so that at the first hint of trading difficulty it collapses. Successful enterprise is difficult enough to come by: it needs the best seedbed and not exposure to biting winds!

The emphasis must be on enabling the regions to help themselves. Outside intervention can be both expensive and counterproductive. The situation in Liverpool shows the failure of successive governments whose policies have merely thrown more and more money at the problem.

Changing local attitudes and removing disincentives is likely to be a better route than massive subsidy. That may mean that government must insist upon communities giving themselves a chance. A national rating system for industry and commerce is an example of this. The electoral temptations of high rates have seduced most of the Labour-controlled councils in the North and Scotland so that in Edinburgh and Sheffield, Liverpool and Manchester, rates on businesses are now a major reason for the loss of jobs and the failure to attract new ones. Rates per square foot in Edinburgh's Princes Street are twenty per cent higher than they are in central London. The John Lewis Partnership faces an enormous disparity in the rating of their premises in Newcastle compared with what they pay in Oxford Street.

There are planning changes as well as urban renewal grants which can do much to make the centres of our cities more attractive to those who would otherwise choose Greenfield sites in the South to build and expand their enterprises. There are many creative ways in which we can redress the balance which history has artificially weighed against some of our older areas. Yet this is the removal of distortion, not the creation of new distortion. Government can use its powers to clear the way for private enterprise and private capital in the recreation of old centres and the opening-up of new opportunities, not just for commerce and industry but for housing and development.

Yet all of this must be carefully monitored lest our desire to be seen to be doing something, the urgency of our Christian concern, blinds us to the danger of the course upon which we are embarked. No company grows great by concentrating on its failures. Investment in success is the key to expansion, and Britain needs expansion. It is our long record of less than average growth which has left us so affected by unemployment.

There is a real limit on the degree to which we dare spend resources on trying to resuscitate the old and outworn instead of concentrating upon the new and innovative. Indeed, part of Britain's continuing problem has been the political imperative to shore up the traditional industries instead of breaking through with the new. People in Liverpool are suffering today, not from the reality of Mrs Thatcher's policies, but from the unreality of all those politicians, trade unionists, managers – yes, and churchmen – who confused charity with sentimentality. They insisted that more and more money be poured into the cities, even though we put £1·5 billion per year into Liverpool alone.

They supported every method to prop up old industry: restrictive practices, protection against imports, regional premiums and special measures. The natural process of industrial death and renewal was held back for years until it was forced upon us in a world recession. Instead of the gradual redeployment of labour, as industry and commerce adjusted to the new conditions over thirty years, we in Britain piled up our problems so that we had a million people who were on the books of companies but nonetheless were in fact unemployed. Companies had allowed over-manning and low productivity to sap their vitality and they had been encouraged and indeed paid to continue to do so. Their uncompetitiveness meant that they were among the least able to withstand the storm as it broke and problems of unemployment and bankruptcy which would have been difficult enough spread over the years became impossible when they came all at once.

Yet it was all intended for the best. Good people had connived at humanitarian solutions which turned out to be vicious. Britain was ill-prepared to meet the recession — ill-prepared by the very people who had sought to do their best to protect the poor from the operation of the market. Out-of-date, out-of-touch and out-of-condition companies collapsed once they had to compete. Yet those very senti-mentalists who stopped Britain doing what Germany and France had done are unrepentant. They still peddle those same policies. They still blame Mrs Thatcher for the results of their own policies. They still claim moral superiority for economic attitudes which have put millions out of work.

The problem is that we find it difficult to take the toughness which alone distinguishes love from sentiment. We see the difference in bringing up our children. So often the answer must be *no* when we yearn to say yes. To say yes because we want it for the child who wants it; yes because we understand that *no* will hurt; or even yes simply because it is easier. Yet good parents have a duty to put backbone into caring. That is what charity is. Caring enough to be tough enough not to give way for temporary advantage. If only we had allowed normal competition to force our industry into the modern world. If only we had restrained the growth of our Welfare State within our ability to pay for it. If only we had invested in success instead of seeking to save failures. Then we should have been prepared enough to survive without the pain of the last seven years.

Primary responsibilities of government

Yet the withdrawal symptoms after too much government intervention must not make us forget the very proper intervening role which governments ought to play. The state has to provide services which cannot be provided by anyone else. The protection of the individual against the assault of his neighbours through the rule of law is perhaps the primary example of this. Parallel to it is that oldest of state responsibilities – the defence of the realm. Law, police, and armed forces are central to the proper role of the state. For the Christian, that role is particularly important because it enables us to defend the poor and the weak.

The rule of law
The breakdown of law and order is much more a threat to those with little muscle than those with great resource. That is why the concept of the rule of law does seem to be a particularly Christian one. We should be very careful at undermining it however strongly we may feel about some special cause. The methods of some Christians in CND and in direct action groups connected with other campaigns are very suspect. By taking the law into their own hands they assert a right which endangers the vulnerable and those most dependent upon the law being upheld. The left's increasing tendency to excuse law-breaking on behalf of what they consider a good cause does not seem to sit easily

with the Christian concern for the poor. It has been used to justify trade unions' refusal to obey Parliament's will and to indemnify councillors who broke the law. Yet, however good the cause, the poor have no security in a society where the more powerful assert their right over the decisions of a democratic Parliament. Christians can have no truck with such action.

Of course, where there is no legitimate government: where the poor have no voice and where law and order is but institutionalized violence in the hands of those who rule, not by Parliament but by force: then the rules are different. How different depends upon the situation. Christians in South Africa and Chile, East Germany and the Soviet Union, Cuba and Ethiopia all have tough decisions to make. The starting-point must be to obey until obedience is impossible. Christian tradition teaches us to respect the law even in the circumstances of a tyrant government. Rendering unto Caesar was applied to an imperial power whose rule was imposed upon an unwilling people. That seems part of our bias to the poor – for the poor rarely gain from revolution and disorder. They are so easily the losers that the Christian ought to be very wary of those who promise secular improvements even in the worst of régimes. Nevertheless the imperative to obey the law is less absolute the less legitimate the régime. Where people can change their governments, convince their fellows, and choose their lawmakers, there is no place for Christian lawbreakers except in the purely personal sense of refusing to obey what conscience forbids. Even then we must accept the sentence of the law as just. A secular society that does not recognize the seal of the confessional may properly imprison the priest who properly refuses to testify. But these are rare examples and always involve the individual refusing to do what he believes to be wrong. It never sanctions the use of deliberate lawbreaking to make a point or advance a cause. Nor does it allow refusal to obey a law which one feels to be mistaken or ill-advised. It is only when a Christian is asked to bow down to idols or to kill babies that he can properly break the law in a democracy.

The defence of the realm

If Christians have a natural bias towards support of law and order, then too we have a proper concern for the defence of the realm. Defending the nation from invasion is part of the defence of freedom and it also must be an extension of the defence of the rule of law. Yet there is a real problem for Christians when faced with the realities of war. There are those who accept the minority pacifist tradition. That is a wholly defensible reaction to the demands of the gospel and does not rely upon any measurement of the horror of particular weapons. For the pacifist war is so clearly opposed to love that a Christian can have no part of it any more than he can be a shareholder in a brothel, hoping thereby to influence the girls for good!

There are those, however, who do not take the pacifist view but nevertheless find it impossible to accept that Christians could be party to the use of weapons of mass destruction. Even a defence policy based upon the threat of such use seems to them inadmissible.

Christians always have a hankering after unilateralism – and not just in defence. It is our most tempting cop-out; our version of 'stop the world, I want to get off'. We look at a world so different from the one God meant; a world where war and tyranny combine to hurt God's children – where hate rules instead of love. We long not to be part of it. We want instead to retreat into God. That desire is an element in our yearning for the Kingdom. Yet desire must not blind us to the reality of what *is*. We have to face up to the question of power in a fallen world. We may wish to be as gentle as doves but that does not excuse us from being as wise as serpents.

We have to start right back with Genesis. The story of the Tree of Knowledge is crucial to the nuclear debate. The problem is the unforgetting nature of man; the Pandora principle. Once we know, we cannot wilfully unknow. Knowledge has therefore to be lived with. So, in a world which knows about nuclear bombs, Christians have to help the world to live with that knowledge. That is the benchmark against which to judge unilateralism.

It is a posture that has to be judged by the simple criterion – does it make nuclear war more or less likely? Does it help the world to live with its knowledge of the Bomb? In making up his mind on that, the Christian has to accept that whatever he decides involves the taking of responsibility. There is no opting out. The unilateralist who, for the highest motives, chooses his way is just as responsible for the results as is the Christian who supports nuclear defence. It is a point which has to be made, for it often appears that those who seek to get rid of nuclear bombs believe the purity of their motives to excuse them from any responsiblity for the consequences of their views and actions.

Unilateral nuclear disarmament would seem to make war more likely. The bully is always attracted by the weak and not the strong and it is difficult to see why that general fact should be found false in the nuclear debate. Countries invade others because they think they are strong enough to win and their enemies weak enough to lose. It is weakness which invites aggression, not strength. In the nuclear context that is particularly important. If we were to accept the socialist defence policy, we should be faced with a potential enemy armed with nuclear weapons against which we have no protection. Where would our conventional weapons then be effective? Russia's threat to drop a bomb cannot be gainsaid. Against her missiles, our tanks can do nothing. We are therefore wholly open to nuclear blackmail as well as the actual use of the Bomb.

And that use cannot be ruled out. The West used nuclear weapons upon Hiroshima and Nagasaki precisely because Japan did not have nuclear weapons. They were the first nuclear-free zones. If Japan had had the ability to retaliate in kind, we should never have dropped the Bomb. So reliance upon conventional weapons in a nuclear world does make nuclear war more likely. It is even more dangerous where the balance of conventional weapons is bound to be so one-sided. A closed society with a huge population and many subject people can use conscription to keep a vast standing army. It can devote a far higher proportion of its GNP to armaments than can a free society whose citizens have real control over spending decisions. The imbalance of conventional weapons in Europe is therefore bound to continue. The aggressor can for this reason be tempted into launching a conventional attack which, once under way, would naturally develop into a nuclear battle if he were repulsed or wanted the short-cut to end the war which so attracted us at Hiroshima.

The Christian tempted by unilateralism must face up to the likely chain of events which his principled stand would set off. He is, of course, not going to be attracted to the Kinnock version of unilateralism which appears to allow Britain to be sheltered by the American nuclear deterrent, while giving up our own and denying the USA any bases here. They would therefore take all the risk, the cost, and the moral obloquy which Labour feels is involved. That cannot be a fit stance for a Christian in whom the principle of personal responsibility looms so large. To pass the buck to the Americans while we wear a halo has more to do with whited sepulchres than Christian witness.

World peace and prosperity

Keeping the peace in a world where nuclear, biological and chemical weapons abound is a task worthy of Christians. We cannot rest when the balance of terror is the only way we have to live with the Bomb. It is within that standoff position that we have to work for reconciliation. It is the Christian gospel which impels us to be peacemakers. Indeed, we should be the pacemakers for peace. Mere denial of the claims of the unilateralists is not enough. We must copy their commitment and their determination. Christians should be the daily reminders of our duty to build bridges and break down divisions in the world. If the Church were really the conscience of the nation it would not allow Mrs Thatcher to rest in her work for peace. The Christian agenda demands that we ought to be pressing her so that no opportunity be lost in the quest for peace.

Yet the cost of avoiding nuclear war is enormous. We are daily reminded of the arms bill and the misuse of our resources in a world in which so many live wretchedly. Yet it is difficult to believe that the price of avoiding war is too great. There is nothing in our experience of the Soviets which would suggest that the world's poor would be better-off if the West laid down its arms and surrendered. Only Western aid and Western trade hold out any hope for the third world. When the Soviet client state Ethiopia exacerbated the drought conditions by its collectivization programme, it was the democracies who had to come to her aid. India gave more food aid than the whole of the Soviet bloc. In practice the developing nations have nothing to hope for from the communist countries materially and everything to fear spiritually.

Increasingly it is being seen that the socialist way is not even suitable for those starting from a very primitive base. It was once a fashionable Christian view that capitalism was not the best way for the new countries who would naturally travel the socialist road and would put up with the disadvantages of control and restriction because they had so much to do and such terrible problems to overcome. In fact, of course, it is all change, even in Africa. Those once committed to central planning and socialist phrases are moving towards economic freedom and even privatization. It is early days yet but the change is there among some of the least likely: Nyerere in Tanzania, Diouf in Senegal and Eyudema in Togo. Socialism is in retreat because it has been found to fail.

The evidence is widespread. China, Hungary, and now even the Soviet Union, have found that socialism does not deliver the goods. They have each turned to capitalist methods to solve their most pressing economic problems. It is therefore not surprising that the third-world countries which have been able to transform the standards of their people and begin to drag themselves up by their bootstraps have used capitalism to do it. Japan, Taiwan, Singapore, South Korea and Hong Kong have all travelled that road.

If, as Christians, we have a real sense of the urgency in improving the life of the poorest in the world, we ought to take seriously the need to promote free societies. There capitalism is most likely to find ways of raising standards and improving conditions. The collectivist is no more successful in changing primitive societies than he is in advanced countries. Perhaps that is because he denies the fundamental human need for choice. It is surely no part of Christianity to palm others off with a system which we would not wish on ourselves!

'Man does not live by bread alone'

Our aid priorities are clear. We must foster the free societies. Instead of food aid which so often undermines the ability of local farmers to become established, we need technical help, suitable tools, simple instruction. Wells and water, primary health care, and the improvement of agriculture are high on the list of our programmes. There is a very great deal to do and much of it will be achieved by the voluntary bodies and the Christian organizations. The more so if the latter were to regain their belief in missionary activity and their real commitment to preaching the gospel.

In the end, the real Christian insight is that it is the hearts of men which have to be changed and that there is no way of achieving that except through the gospel of Jesus Christ. Yet we too have become infected by the materialist creed. The Christian overseas effort in Britain is no longer spearheaded by the missionary societies but by Christian Aid and Oxfam. We do not generally have the same enthusiasm for preaching the gospel to all nations but rather have substituted the good-hearted determination to do what we can about the underdevelopment of some nations.

It is of course a Christian duty voluntarily to give to the poor. It is also a Christian duty to preach the gospel. Perhaps it is an index of our own uncertainties about the truth of the Christian faith that we are much less determined today about the latter. They should go hand in hand. Meeting the material needs of developing nations is the concomitant and not the substitute for meeting their spiritual needs.

Now that may seem like a Christian insider argument; a question of the Churches' priorities. Yet it raises the issue which lies at the heart of the whole debate about the Church and politics. The Church has a right to be heard only if it is true to the gospel. It is the uniqueness of the revelations of God to man in the birth, death and resurrection of Jesus Christ, that gives the Church any standing at all. The problem for many politicians is their real suspicion that the fervour for the faith which should characterize the Church has been replaced by a generalized good-heartedness which turns Christianity into a pressure group for government spending on good causes.

Living by the demands of the gospel

And here Christians do have to face up to a real difficulty in the stance which equates Christian concern for the poor with the demand for government action. The gospel is about individual voluntary action, not about corporate compulsory provision. Indeed, the emphasis is on the importance of giving to the giver rather than the receiver. In the New Testament the young man is told to go away and give all that he has to the poor for his own good rather than that of the poor. The Church has therefore to be careful in bringing the gospel demands up to date. One of the real difficulties of giving by proxy is that it turns giving into a matter only of the receiver. When Christians campaign for higher taxation to fund greater government spending on social security, there are some real economic consequences which we shall come to later. Yet there is also a very real religious concern. The widow *gave* her two mites, she was not assessed two mites for tax purposes. There is a freedom in Christian giving which makes it sit uneasily with compulsory taxation. That is not to deny the right of a state to take money from its citizens to spend on the poor. It is merely to warn against the easy identification of gospel injunctions about the poor with a particular view about the maintainance and extension of the British welfare state. There is no direct read-over. There is nothing in the gospel which should make it a Christian duty to favour high taxation and pervasive state welfare provision. There is much in the gospel which warns against the dangers of riches and insists on the need for stewardship.

So the first priority of the Church is to set the importance of freewill offering before its faithful. When the Catholic Apostolic Church rediscovered the value of tithing in the nineteenth century, it was its effect upon the Christian life of its giving members rather than the financial advantage to church funds which was noteworthy! We might learn that again today. Yet, having reasserted the place of Christian stewardship, does the Church have a further insight which can properly lead it to demand compulsory giving, through taxation, for causes of which it approves?

Here we really do have to face up to conflicting economic theories as well as trying to reconcile different Christian priorities. The Conservative would say that we must not allow taxation levels to rise so that they inhibit enterprise, drive talent abroad and reduce the nation's potential wealth. This view is not held in order to protect the rich, the able and the advantaged. It is necessary if we are to create enough wealth to see to the needs of the poor, the disabled and the disadvantaged. Now particular Christians may not agree with the economic analysis which informs the Tory view. That disagreement cannot, however, be a matter of morality. It is an economic argument on which it is perfectly possible for Christians to disagree. Their ends – the bettering of the conditions of the least able in society – remain the same. Their human judgement on the methods of achieving those ends differ as much as do those of Buddhists or humanists.

'But', say some Christians, 'it isn't right that a few should be very very rich!' It is some 'soft' socialists' view that no one should earn more than three times the average wage. One can feel the attraction of this contention but it is very muddle-headed. What we ought to be concerned about is what the rich person does with his riches and not what those riches amount to. If you want a vibrant society which is able to make the most of people's potential then you must allow the market to place money value upon particular talents. After all, the man with ten talents was commended for making them twenty. What the Christian has to say is about the use of those talents and what he has to warn of is about their dangers.

Christians have nothing to say as Christians about the level of taxation but a great deal to say about the personal responsibility of the rich for their riches. The idea that a society is necessarily better because it makes it impossible for people to earn or to own much more than the average has no Christian basis. It is a conception which springs from envy. Indeed, one of the root causes for Britain's decline has been that we have had a political structure in which one party has built its electoral appeal upon envy. And what a cramping and cribbing sin envy is! It is the business of begrudging others their good fortune or the fruits of their hard work. It is summed up in the old story to illustrate the difference between Britain and the USA. In New York, a man walking down Park Avenue sees another in a huge Cadillac and his automatic response is 'Someday I'll have one of those.' His British counterpart, walking down Park Lane, sees a man in a Rolls-Royce pass by and his immediate reaction is 'One day we'll have him out of there.'

Now the man on the pavement in London would not be one whit better off if there were no Rolls-Royces – indeed, he might well be more likely to be unemployed. The man on the sidewalk in New York, on the other hand, has already taken the first step in improving his lot. Christians may want to question the priorities of those who choose big cars but our religion does not demand that we insist upon putting them down by law.

Yet there are some distinctive marks which characterize a Christian view of society. Because we hold so centrally the distinct worth of each human being, then we do want to enable people to fulfil their potential. Opportunity is again the key. We have a presumption therefore to give more people more chance to make more of their own lives for themselves. We accept that part of that must be to allow people to make their own mistakes and we fear the tendency of some social engineers to want to manage people's lives for them. The 'food-stamps' approach seems alien to Christian thought. We cannot easily favour a system designed to protect people from their own follies. To demean people just because they are on social security runs counter to any commitment to equality of worth.

Help for the deprived should be designed to build up their independence rather than merely to make them financially closer to the average. High welfare payments which make men and women more dependent are morally debilitating. Those who believe that their problems can only be solved by someone else and are in no way their own responsibility, are made less human. The cycle of deprivation is exactly that. Generation succeeding generation, secure in the belief that the state must provide, for they have no need nor duty to do so. These are human beings in whom the image of God has been dulled by dependence. The Christian does not advance the Kingdom at all by promoting such a welfare state. Instead he ought to seek a system which encourages people into independence: a system which makes working decidedly more attractive than not working; one which expects of the able-bodied, community service as the natural repayment for unemployment benefit; and one which gives benefits in cash rather than kind in order that even the poorest may choose. Such a system is of course a safety net and not a hammock. It is in a hurry to encourage people to find a better way of securing their futures. It is constantly under tension between the need to provide and the necessity of ensuring that that provision does not make for dependence. The Christian will therefore not always be popular in his attitudes. There will be a toughness in place of sentimentality; a concern that men should not lose the dignity of contribution. That is because the Christian is deeply aware that material prosperity makes it *more* difficult to enter the Kingdom of heaven. Because he knows that man does not live by bread alone, he is determined that the welfare system should not encourage people to believe that man does. So the 'cradle to the grave' concept is approached with considerable scepticism by men and women whose permissible dependence is upon God who will call them to account.

This is no comfortable creed because it depends upon a commitment to the personal demands of the gospel. The challenge is very plain. Jesus identifies himself with the starving: 'When I hungered, you gave me not to eat.' The responsibility is on us. It cannot be passed to the state or left to someone else. Passing by on the other side is no more excusable in a welfare state than it is in a society without community provision.

Living by a code of personal morality

And the Christian agenda is not the world's. Even though we have our fellow travellers among those who do not share our faith, we have an attitude to the individual which makes demands upon us as upon few non-Christians. We are not the prisoners of some fateful system. We are our own men and women, responsible for our own actions. We were created by a God who loves us and allows us to share in his creative activity. In being born into a human family he characterized it as divine. He made man in his own image and enabled man to make others in that divine image. At the heart of our relationship with God is love, and at the heart of our closest human relationships we find that love too. It is therefore not surprising that Christians have always seen sexual morality as something which cannot be treated lightly. Even at a time when modernists among theologians have moved close to situational ethics and away from absolutes, the teaching of the Church as it is generally understood has upheld the traditional moral codes. Now as AIDS gives us a sharp reminder that the easy sex of the birth-control, gender-bending era turns out to have deadly drawbacks, clergymen are beginning again to underscore publicly the moral absolutes of the Church's teaching.

Many aspects of this teaching are not directly the concern of government. The law has proved an ineffective moral policeman. Yet some issues press hard upon the Christian conscience of the politician.

Last year we killed 150,000 unborn babies largely for the convenience of their parents. We did so with a national collective amnesia which is terrifying. The largest mass lobby of Parliament went unreported by radio and television and by almost every newspaper. Abortion is best forgotten. It is uncomfortable if too closely considered. What a challenge to Christian politicians – committed to defend the weak. We who have a special responsibility to protect those who cannot protect themselves. We are not here enforcing a moral code about which there is a real debate in a secular society. We are facing up to a direct challenge to the sanctity of human life and human life at its most vulnerable. It is Parliament which has allowed abortion and it is Parliament which must stop it. What an irony it is that we have legalized abortion at the very point in human history when we are most able to prevent conception at will. In a sense we have been led to overturn the moral code of centuries at the point when it is least oppressive.

In seeking to defend the defenceless, Christians are bound to refer to the moral code which the Church teaches and to which we seek to live. It is never an easy thing to do, not least because each one of us is all too conscious of our own failings and shortcomings. The fear of hypocrisy is rightly with us always. Yet the urgency of respect for God's law cannot be ignored by Christians in or out of politics. God does not insist upon a set of arbitrary rules, but upon obedience to him because that is the way in which we are delivered from evil. The Church teaches a moral code which enables us to act as nature intended and not as fallen man desires. The current concern about AIDS illustrates this only too dramatically. It is a scourge which we have brought upon ourselves and it is one which we spread by our own actions. It is not God's wrath which pursues us, for he is not a vengeful God. Instead it is his justice. It is the inevitable result of our refusal to obey. We were not willing to accept the law which alone can deliver us from evil.

In trying to see how Christianity works through our political life, we are bound to be concerned, not just with the great issues of peace and war, of social justice and world development. We have too to be concerned with the individual matters of human morality. There is much here which Parliament cannot control, although it may influence. We cannot make men good but we must act as if we thought that goodness mattered. For too long we have seemed to be impartial about right and wrong when it concerned personal morality. We have set no standards and we have sought to uphold no examples. A society now threatened by AIDS can properly ask what its politicians did when the 1960s permissive wave broke over us. The weak and the vulnerable received precious little help then. As one in three marriages now end in divorce and the single-parent family becomes an increasing concern of almost every department of social welfare, society has a right to feel let down by the politicians who paved the legal way for sequential marriage and provided the welfare benefits to pay for it.

Politics is not enough!

The hunger of those who look up for a shepherd cannot be satisfied by politicians. It is the hunger of the whole individual which can only be satisfied by the gospel of Jesus Christ. Politicians have pretended that they could satisfy human needs to far greater an extent than could ever be possible. This is the real false promise of the politician. He promised he could rescue the world from the facts of life. He offered controls and direction in economic life by which he thought he could get round the laws of supply and demand and manage the effects of the market. He embraced the revolt against the natural law and removed the signposts and safeguards which society had erected to help men and women order their personal and sexual morality. He has pretended to too much power and has played God.

The Christian politician must learn again the bounds of his remit. We shall not bring about the Kingdom of God by the action of the state. That Kingdom comes in the hearts of men and women. It is they who turn to him. We can help to foster the conditions in which they may more readily respond to the gospel through the priorities which we set and the agenda which we lay down. Our respect for human personality and individual worth will be the benchmark by which we are judged. It will influence our views on pornography as much as on privatization. It will make us more willing to 'trust the people' than to believe that 'the man in Whitehall knows best'. It will drive us from the politics of envy towards those of opportunity. It will make us use the engine of capitalism in order to provide the means for social justice. We shall be concerned at the personal example which we set and the signals which our lawmaking sends out. We shall have to face up to the Christian implications of a welfare state which discourages work and enables the increasing breakdown of the family.

Christians are not easy bedfellows in any political party and they are clearly not confined to any one. What does seem true is that the underlying analysis of society and the scope of politics presented by the Conservative Party is one which many Christians find closest to what the Gospels would lead us to expect from a government fundamentally influenced by Christian principles.

Part Two

The Case for Labour

ERIC HEFFER

Christian principles and British socialism

As I write, it is clear that the decks are slowly but surely being cleared for a General Election. The timing of such an election is of course in the hands of the Prime Minister; so no one, perhaps not even the PM herself, can be certain when it will take place. Under present political circumstances, there will be three main contestants: the Conservatives; the Labour Party; and the SDP/Liberal Alliance, which will be fighting the election on a joint ticket, though the two parties disagree with one another on some quite fundamental issues.

Among members of these political parties there are professed Christians who make no secret of their religious beliefs. No doubt they will claim that their particular views deserve the support of those voters who are also Christians. Mrs Thatcher very much makes her appeal to Christian voters, and I shall never forget the picture of her standing outside No. 10 Downing Street reading aloud the prayer of St Francis. I thought then, and think now, that it was a cheek for her to recite that prayer, suggesting that she was guided by its sentiments, when in fact she was advocating confrontation rather than peace.

Mrs Thatcher, like others in the Tory Party, argues passionately that her policies are based on a Christian outlook. They certainly are, if one accepts the definition of Christianity as believing that Jesus lived, that he was the Son of God and performed miracles. But Christianity is surely something more than that. It is not just a ticket for one's personal salvation in heaven; it is accepting a commitment to be on the side of the poor, to support the oppressed, to oppose the rich and powerful and to recognize that we are our brothers' and our sisters' keepers. It is the belief that the 'Kingdom of God' should be worked for and created here on earth.

Stated in those terms, Christian principles are also the basic perspectives of British socialism, and therefore Labour Party members, whether religious or not, can accept Christ's teachings as basically their own. In working for a Labour government with socialist objectives they are also accepting the Christian idea of creating God's Kingdom.

Keir Hardie, a founder of the Labour Party, rightly said: 'When the old civilizations were putrefying, the still small voice of Jesus the Communist stole over the earth like a soft, refreshing breeze carrying healing wherever it went.'

The religious roots of the Labour movement

The important thing to remember about Christianity is that it is an umbrella movement. Beneath that umbrella shelter all kinds of organized churches, sects, groups (some large, some small), all claiming to be Christian.

In Britain we have the Roman Catholic Church, which was the first Christian Church here, even though it was divided and had to be united at the first Synod of the Church ever held in this country – in my native town of Hertford. There is the established state Church, the Church of England, which was the direct result of the break with Rome by Henry VIII and, of course, later there developed the multifarious dissident churches which grew out of the reformation in both Scotland and England and which in some cases directly arose out of the 1640 English Revolution.

The struggle for the vote, for the People's Charter, also had some religious input.

It is interesting to note that one of the Chartist insignia not only has the words 'This is our Charter' inscribed on it, but also 'God is our guide'. In some parts of the country, Chartist chapels were established and some of those who preached on Chartism were Methodists. Other Chartist preachers belonged to other denominations.

Dorothy Thompson, in her book *The Chartists*, quotes a Mr Rushton who spoke at Littletown Chapel in the Spen

Valley. He had as one of his texts: 'The poor ye have always with you.' He argued that there were three classes of poor. There were God's poor, the maim and blind; there were the poor made so by reckless living, and who had put themselves in that position by their own actions; and there were the poor who, despite having worked hard all their lives, had been made poor or kept poor because of oppressive actions by others, who had deprived them of their God-given rights.

Rushton argued that it was a sin that some people lorded over others in an unjust way and that the misery of the poor resulted from the actions of the rich and powerful.

Those who argue that religion, i.e. Christianity, has nothing to do with politics, are either speaking out of ignorance or consciously repudiating British and other church history, usually for their own political ends. Politics and political involvement have always been part of Christianity. Political struggles of the past were carried out within the Church and were part of the argument against the hierarchy of the various Churches of the times.

With regard to political struggles in the House of Commons reflecting the struggles in the country, Christians took opposite sides. They still do.

There was, for example, a small group of MPs which included Wilberforce, who believed strongly in the abolition of slavery. Those MPs acted as a group and were referred to by writers, later, as the Clapham Sect. In their own day they were known as 'the Saints'.

They were not trying to change society fundamentally. They were not socialists, but they were trying to give the society in which they lived a human face. They worked to get rid of its worst excesses. They, or at least some of them, did not always see the exploitation of the working people in Britain. Instead, they concentrated on oppressed peoples abroad, and campaigned particularly vigorously against slavery.

As far as the Church of England was concerned, there

were those within the Church who demanded that it should restore its Catholicism. The Tractarians Pusey and Newman gave the Church its Anglo-Catholicism. However, they did not always see the need to take sides on what in those days was called the 'Social Question' and instead concentrated on internal church matters. As C. E. Raven said in his *Christian Socialism*, 'When the cry of the oppressed was ringing in men's ears and when Christians might have listened to the prophets of social righteousness or to the victims of social evil, fifty years were wasted in lawsuits over "regeneration" and ritual, vestments and incense and the precise meaning of sixteenth-century values'.

In effect, the Tractarians repudiated the new materialism of the capitalist system — not by challenging it but by ignoring it.

The work of people such as the Rev. Stewart Headlam should not be underestimated. Born in 1847, he founded the Guild of St Matthew, and was editor of the *Church Reformer*. He was active politically; and was a member of the London School Board from 1888 to 1904, and of the London County Council from 1907. Headlam and other churchmen were active in helping to create the Fabian Society.

Fabian Tract No. 78 by the Rev. John Clifford, published in May 1898, was called 'Socialism and the Teaching of Christ'. In it he argues: 'Christian men are agreeing more and more, (*a*) in their antagonism to individual greed and injustice, (*b*) in personal and sympathetic devotion to the welfare of the people; the parting of the ways is (*c*) as the real basis on which modern industry shall organize itself.'

He states that some consider it 'anti-Christ' when socialists say: '(*a*) Our industrial life should be based not on individuals but on collective ownership of the chief elements and material instruments of production; (*b*) that production should be managed not according to the will or caprice or might of private individuals, but collectively; and (*c*) that the results of toil should be distributed to all who have a share in the toil on the principles of absolute justice, i.e. on the principle of equality in action.'

He answers by pointing out that Christ said: 'Lay not up for yourselves treasures on earth'; and that 'man's life consists not in the abundance of things he possesses but in the use he makes of what he has – if for himself – still for himself not as an end, but as a means for promoting the well-being of the world.'

Sir Thomas More, the author of *Utopia*, has a brass plaque to his memory in Westminster Hall at the Palace of Westminster. He was once Chancellor and his struggles against Henry VIII, which were both Christian and political, led to his martyrdom. King Charles I was undoubtedly a Christian, but was condemned to death by other Christians. The rise to power of the merchants, bankers and traders was political, but the arguments were conducted in religious terms. Even to this day, as long as the Church of England is the Established Church, then certain church issues needing the imprint of legislation come before Parliament, and can be debated and voted upon by MPs who are not Christians, or even if they are, are not necessarily members of the Church of England. Politics, therefore, are involved in church affairs, and on the other side of that coin, Christian values and concepts are essentially part of the political struggle.

Take for example issues such as abortion. Christians are divided on this question. While many are anti-abortion, others take a less strict view and give what is described as a balanced response. Certainly, high regard for human life is a major Christian concept and it is important to work to safeguard it, but under certain circumstances – for example, if one life is to be given up for another – then the argument becomes complicated. The same can be said with regard to scientific experiments. Christians do differ on such issues and can find biblical quotations to support practically any point of view. I often wish I had the arrogance of certainty. Then I would not be torn by doubts as I am now, by seeing both sides of an argument, rather than – like some – believing that only one viewpoint is correct. I suppose one should always try to maintain principles but aim to be flexible within those principles.

Can we then have Christian principles in politics? It is an important question, and one which I believe can be answered in the affirmative.

As I said earlier, Christians have different attitudes to issues, to society, and that is because they, like everyone else, are part of their own cultural environment. One can either accept one's environment and make the most of it, or seek to change it. At the beginning of his book, *Religion and the Rise of Capitalism*, R. H. Tawney quotes Bishop Berkeley, who said: 'Whatever the world thinks, he who hath not much meditated upon God, the human mind, and the Summum Bonum, may possibly make a thriving earthworm, but will indubitably make a sorry patriot and a sorry statesman.'

The truth of the matter is that all great men and women who have had an impact on the world's thinking, have thought much about the idea of God and the human mind, even when they have not accepted the reality of God. Karl Marx was undoubtedly someone who gave great thought to God and religion. His phrase, 'religion is the opium of the people', has more than once been taken out of its context.

From its early days the Labour Movement in Britain had a quasi-religious aspect: for instance, in the socialist ten commandments issued by the Aberdare Branch of the Independent Labour Party. They were designed for the children who attended the socialist Sunday School. They are: '(1) Love your schoolfellows, who will be your fellow workmen in life; (2) Love learning, which is the food of the mind; be as grateful to your teacher as to your parents; (3) Make every day a holy day by good and useful deeds and kindly actions; (4) Honour good men, be courteous to all men, bow down to none; (5) Do not hate or speak evil of anyone. Do not be revengeful, but stand up for your rights and resist oppression; (6) Do not be cowardly. Be a friend to the weak and love justice; (7) Remember that all the good things on the earth are produced by labour. Whoever enjoys them without working for them is stealing the bread of the workers; (8) Observe and think in order to discover the truth. Do not believe what is contrary to reason, and never deceive yourself or others; (9) Do not think that he who loves his own country must hate and despise other nations, or wish for war which is a remnant of barbarism; (10) Look forward to the day when all men will be free citizens as brothers in peace and righteousness.'

The statement ends with a dedication: 'We desire to be just and loving to all our fellow men and women, to work together as brothers and sisters, to be kind to every living creature and so help to form a new society, with Justice and Love as its foundation, and LOVE ITS LAW.'

To me, these statements are basically Christian and although I did not go to a socialist Sunday School, I did go to a Church of England Sunday School. I was taught very much the same precepts, so Christianity and socialism were to me something similar, not opposites.

Obviously, the growth of capitalism had its champions in the Protestant sects. Calvinism, in particular, became the accepted religion of the many capitalist entrepreneurs. Nevertheless, it should not be forgotten that Calvinists in Geneva at the time of Calvinist control were very much against the sin of avarice. As Tawney says, 'The capitalist who borrowed in order to invest and make a profit could take care of himself . . . The crucial issue was that of the money-lender who makes advances . . . and who thereby exploits the necessities of his poorer neighbours.'

Such people were railed against. The interesting thing is that the position still holds today. Many Christians who are Tories accept that making a profit is perfectly acceptable, but that to lend money and make money, at the expense of the poor, is not. What they fail to understand is that it is the very system which is wrong, and what is required is a fundamental change in the system – not just some tinkering around with controls in the City to stop the worst abuses, but a society where such an institution as the City would be superfluous.

Working for the collective good

The religion of the Thatcherite Tories is basically Protestant in the Calvinist sense of putting the individual first. But if we reject the idea that the individual is all-important, we do not deny that the individual is important in the context of the collectivity of society as a whole. In other words, we accept that society must be the collective expression of free individuals working together for the good of all and not just for themselves. And if we accept this, we accept that the socialist, Labour idea is important.

It is important to have a National Health Service which takes the fear out of illness and concentrates on getting the patient well without the worry of whether or not the treatment can be paid for.

It is important that we should have a Social Security system which abolishes poverty and removes the fear from the old of being put into workhouses; and in which the sick and disabled know that they will get a fair deal and will be protected and not allowed to starve.

It is important that people should be employed, have a secure job and know that they cannot be dismissed easily by a profit-hungry employer, who is not concerned with safety and health at work but who wishes to use young people and women as cheap labour.

It is important that everyone should have a decent home in which to live, with security of tenure, with rents or repayments which can be afforded without hardship. It is important that homes should have the proper amenities, and be safe and habitable.

It is important that people should have a good education, that children be given every opportunity to go further up the educational ladder without hardship and by right. It is wrong that some, because of birth, power and privilege, receive a good education and have their life prospects assured for them, while others with ability are held back because of their environment and lack of finance.

It is important that the nation's capital and material resources should be used by the people in the interests of the people as a whole and not cornered by some for profit at the expense of the weak. That is why our system of production must be publicly owned, properly planned, and with the workers by hand and by brain jointly running the industries.

It is important that working people should have a right to belong to free and independent trade unions, free from state control, with the members running their own affairs, electing their own officials and generally controlling their unions through democratic practices. It is right that anti-trade union laws should be removed from the Statute Book and laws introduced to restore to the unions their previous rights, with additional rights to organize, etc.

It is right and important to fight for peace, to keep war at bay, to get rid of nuclear weapons and eventually to work for all destructive weapons to be abolished in all countries.

These are all, basically, Labour's objectives. They are something the Labour Movement works towards, and they are also in my view Christian proposals that are based on the early ideas of the Church. No doubt it will be argued that there are Christians in the SDP/Liberal Alliance – that they too advance Christian ideas. It will rightly be pointed out that Dr David Owen is a Christian, as is Mrs Shirley Williams, although they belong to different denominations. No one doubts their belief in Christ or the Church to which they belong. As I said earlier, all Christians do not think alike, and they have different attitudes towards Christianity. Individuals can be either selfish or not selfish. They can be good and bad at the same time; and in politics they also differ. Politicians can advocate some excellent proposals inside an overall programme which is not helpful to society.

While I am sure many will not agree with me, I believe

British politics are based on class. The Tory Party stands for and on behalf of the Big Business interests. Mrs Thatcher and her colleagues have pursued their brand of politics because they agree with the capitalist system, with private ownership of all industry, with individual advancement as against collective advancement and with Victorian values of thrift and hard work.

In such a philosophy, the old, sick and infirm, the inadequate and unfortunate, the poor and humble, get pushed aside and the rich and wealthy do very well. To me, despite the profession of Christianity on the part of many Tories, I believe this to be an anti-Christian philosophy.

With regard to the SDP/Liberal Alliance, they are by no means a homogeneous whole. In many respects, Dr Owen reflects the view of the Tories. He advocates the Social Market, which is little different from what Mrs Thatcher advocates. In both the SDP and Liberal Parties there are some who are more radical and still have views which, if put into effect, would help some of the poor as well as the struggle for peace.

The SDP, however, is not a Labour Party. Like the Liberal Party it is a quasi-Conservative Party and, again, I find their ideas in many respects contrary to what I believe to be the basic ideas of Christianity. It is my view that those who are Christian, who are genuinely biased towards the poor, who are against nuclear weapons and who do believe in the collective good as against selfish individualism, should join the Labour Party and help keep Labour a truly socialist Party.

Over recent years a dialogue has been developing between Christians and Marxists. It is a dialogue that should be encouraged. They have a lot to learn from each other, especially as in Britain the division between the two has never been as deep as in some other countries.

There is not and never has been a religious test for individuals when joining the Labour Party. People of any religion or no religion can join, as can people of all nationalities. Its basic position is outlined in Clause IV, Part IV of the Party Constitution: that is, the common ownership of the means of production, distribution and exchange with the best possible popular control.

Today, Labour's objective is still the establishment of a socialist society. Labour still stands for bringing an end to some privatization, for a moderate extension of public ownership, for the removal of US nuclear bases and British nuclear weapons. It is calling for the repeal of anti-trade union legislation, with some new laws to be substituted. The policy being put forward is not as strong in socialist terms as in 1983 or 1979. Despite that, the Tories are insisting that the policy is more socialist than it is and are trying to give the impression that Labour intends to create some sort of East European state. It is with that concept that they hope to frighten the electorate.

The idea of Christians and Marxists working together to create a new society, and what is involved in this, was put clearly by Paul Ostreicher, who in his book *Dialogue of Christianity and Marxism* said: 'I have not ventured beyond this world. For this I make no apology. It is not because my readers are likely to be mainly atheist. It is because Jesus should have left his Church in no doubt that love of men is our only legitimate business. Loving God is only possible by loving men. "What you do – or fail to do – for a man, you do – or fail to do – for God." And that puts believers and non-believers on a level. Actions alone count. Theories are only relevant if they lead to action for *men*. This world is the only possible place for such action.'

That is so true. A Christian and a Socialist can be one and the same. Socialists who are not Christians, who are materialists, may well be better 'Christians' in practice than some who call themselves Christians. All can take political action, join the Labour Party and become involved in working for a Labour government which it is hoped will advance socialist policies.

Christ the revolutionary

I carry around at all times the prayer which says, 'God, grant me the serenity to accept the things I cannot change . . . courage to change the things I can, and wisdom to know the difference'. There are, of course, some things that, try as I may, I cannot change. But most things can be changed, if only marginally. I believe that Christians must change society for the better, that they can help to change it fundamentally and in the process bring about the 'Kingdom of God' on earth.

That is the view long held by various people in the Labour Movement in Britain. Not just clergy, but lay people in particular. The British Labour Movement, unlike many European labour movements, has not been fundamentally anti-religious, although it has always had in its ranks some who were. That, however, goes for most political movements in Britain. Rationalists and atheists are by no means confined to Labour or socialism. Although in Britain Marxism has never had complete domination in the Labour Movement, it has undoubtedly greatly influenced it, primarily because politics in Britain are class politics – and whatever the SDP/Liberal Alliance may say to the contrary, they still are.

Christianity itself has never been totally homogeneous, despite becoming powerful and identified too often with state establishments. It has had and continues to have various currents within it, one of which has never been identified with the ruling-class establishment, and which has been revolutionary in character and outlook, identifying itself with Christ the carpenter.

Jesus was undoubtedly a revolutionary. He was classified as a subversive by the state functionaries of his day. He wanted to change and improve society and was against oppression of all kinds. His disciples were basically poor men who can be described in modern parlance as 'ordinary men'. They too were considered subversive. Conrad Noel, whose writings have affected me considerably, wrote a book

56

called *Jesus the Heretic*. In Noel's view Jesus was crucified for political and theological heresy as well as for being the Son of God. I believe that, and I therefore identify Christianity as the movement to change things. Persecution of those who fight for a decent and better society is therefore to be expected, as that in fact is what happened to Christ. It is my view that Christianity and socialism are working for the same ends, i.e. a world where greed and selfishness are things of the past, where power will reside among the people and not be centralized in the hands of one person or small groups, where poverty will be abolished and privilege for a few ended for all time.

How can this be done? Can it be achieved on the basis of the present capitalist mode of production – that is, production for profit and not for use? Surely, it is the very system of private ownership of the means of production, the drive for profits, which creates the selfish society, a society which places individual greed above society as a whole and where competition rather than co-operation between people is considered normal and rational. The capitalist system with its competitiveness is the opposite of the Christian view that 'I am my brother's keeper'.

The socialist idea is also very much part of the Jewish Old Testament. In fact, socialism, in the shape of a struggle of the lower classes in society to raise up their conditions, is as old as history itself. Moses put forward the need to prevent inequality among the tribes of Israel, and private property and inheritance was sanctioned only under strict conditions. In Leviticus a system of landholding was proposed which was intended to provide reasonable equality. A remarkable institution, the Jubilee, was also introduced (Leviticus ch. 25).

The Law of Moses was essentially a type of socialism. The Old Testament prophets constantly argued for a return to the ideas of Moses, i.e. basic socialist ideas, and Isaiah was undoubtedly the strongest of them all.

Christ carried on the ideas of the prophets. The poor were

to be exalted and the rich brought down. There should be no private property and no competition. Everyone was to do the greatest good for all. Christian teaching was that one should serve others and not expect anything in return. The important thing to remember is that Christ believed such a society could be created here on earth.

The Labour Party's socialist view of society is, in my view, basically a Christian view – certainly as put forward by the founder of Christianity, Jesus himself.

In his book *Christianity at the Crossroads* Jon Sobrino SJ puts what is described as a Latin-American view. His book is dedicated to Father Grande SJ and Fr Alfonso Navarro, whom he describes as martyrs for the Kingdom of God in El Salvador.

Father Sobrino argues strongly that it was sin which brought about the death of the Son of God. 'Today, then, sin is that which brings death to the children of God, to human beings; it may be sudden, violent death, or it may be the slow, unremitting death caused by unjust structures. This leads us to a different view of the insistent emphasis on Christ as the embodiment of universal reconciliation, which is ingenuously preached by some and defended by others out of self-interest. Such an emphasis is nothing else but an attempt to exempt Jesus from the conflict-ridden tools of history, to use Christianity as a support for some sort of ideology espousing peace and order and as a weapon against any kind of conflict or subversion.'

He goes on to make the point that that 'is an attempt to keep Christians strangers to the sinfulness and conflictual nature of history. When Christians do get involved in the conflicts of history they can simply be accused of being subversives and phoney Christians.'

How true all that is. In Britain today, certainly since the Church of England produced its report on nuclear weapons, and on the situation in the cities, the cry from some Conservative MPs and others who are members of the Church has been that the Church should keep out of politics and concentrate on the saving of individual souls. It is an old cry, and fits nicely into the pattern of ideas of the ruling establishment in society who do not want people to try to change things, but to submit to what we have now and rest content with capitalism until they die and hopefully enter the Kingdom of heaven.

But Christians should not be content. They should be as Jesus was, dissatisfied with the society in which they live. They should spend time and energy on trying to change society in a positive direction on behalf of the 'ordinary people'. Although it has been suggested that the words were inserted later, Flavius Josephus in his *Jewish Antiquities* written at the period of the Roman conquest of Israel, said in Book 20, chapter 9.1, that 'James, the brother of Jesus, said to be the Christ, together with some others, was brought to court, accused as a breaker of the law and delivered over to be stoned to death'. So the early Christians were considered to be 'breakers of the law', and they were not only a relative minority in society, they were also made up largely of the poor. In the main they were uneducated peasants and artisans. For quite a long time the Christian communities did not attract the upper classes. It was only in the middle and towards the end of the second century AD that this happened.

Christianity at first, therefore, was basically the religion of the poor and the oppressed, of the 'subversives', and because of that they were persecuted, killed and crucified. Later, as has happened so often in the past, the movement of the poor was taken over by the establishment and in some countries it became a pillar of the state. It happened to Christianity in Rome and to Marxism in Moscow. From that point onwards, the revolutionary nature of the religion was lost sight of, and to a large extent it became transformed into its opposite. That is why in Britain for a long time it was said that the Church of England, the state establishment religion, was the Tory Party at prayer. The Tories still foster this myth, as is often shown at Tory Party conferences.

Despite this, there have always been currents and elements within the Church of England, in fact in all Christian Churches, which have not accepted the establishment view and who have sided with the poor and the oppressed and have spoken out for them – sometimes putting themselves at the head of the struggle to change society on behalf of working people.

The Labour Party has always included in its ranks good socialists who have been Christians. A considerable number have been left-wing socialists, for example John Wheatley, George Lansbury, Sir Stafford Cripps, Lord Soper. Others in the Labour Movement, such as James Connolly, the Irish revolutionary socialist, remained true to their religion, as well as to their socialism, to the day they died.

Such socialists did not see their religion as something apart from their socialism, but as indivisible, the one complementary to the other. That is a view I personally hold. To fight for a socialist Britain as part of a socialist world, is, I believe, part of my Christian heritage. Christian concepts of co-operation, of working for the common good, of opposing oppression, of standing up for truth and against evil, are the concepts upon which the socialist ideal is based.

The great William Temple, who for the short period of two and a half years was Archbishop of Canterbury, argued most strongly against those who said the Church should not become involved in politics. From 1920 to 1927 he edited a journal called *The Pilgrim*. Later, many of his essays from that journal were reprinted in a book, *Essays on Christian Politics*. In it he said: 'No firm line can be drawn marking off those sides of public life ... which properly concern the Church from those which do not.' He also said: 'Just because of its concern with individual character, the Church is vitally concerned with the conditions that affect that character.'

How true are these words. People are products of their environment. Today we have a society which puts individual greed and selfishness above the interests of society as a whole. It is not suggested by the ideologists of the existing capitalist system that the interests of the individual are served best by the elevation and protection of all, but precisely the opposite, with the individual coming *before* society as a whole. We have media coverage and TV programmes that increasingly appeal to the worst features of individual greed. The 'look after yourself: to hell with everyone else' philosophy of 'I'm all right, Jack' is now the dominant one in Britain. It has been particularly visible since the election of the Thatcher governments, which encourage individualism rather than the collective good.

William Temple preached the reverse of present-day social values and urged Christians to work for something different, when he said that Christianity must 'criticize actual institutions in the light of its own social principles, because it aims, not at the salvation of individuals one by one, but at that perfect individual and social welfare, which is called the Kingdom of God or the Holy City'.

I believe we must strive to build the Kingdom of God. It can only be built in modern terms if we use all the tools available, and that means using some of the theoretical instruments of other beliefs as well as those of Christianity itself. There has to be a synthesis which Christians must accept. It would be wrong to say that everyone must accept Christian ideas; they do not, and never will, but that should not stop people who are Christians working with others who are not, for the good of all. The objectives of many non-Christians are clearly the same as those of Christians; they too want to build the 'Kingdom of God' on earth, but would not call it that, or even recognize it as such once it was created. It would still be such a 'Kingdom' nevertheless.

The arguments used against William Temple by Tory politicians are similar to those used against the Archbishop of Canterbury and other bishops today.

In 1934, William Temple wrote to *The Times* urging Neville Chamberlain, then Chancellor of the Exchequer with his promised financial surplus, not to decrease income tax but to restore cuts which had been made on unemployment benefit. He received a very sharp rejoinder from Chamberlain who said: 'When I read that letter I thought it was a pity that the Archbishop should suggest, as it seems to me he did by implication, that MPs require to be reminded of humanitarian feelings which otherwise would not occur to them.'

The Archbishop was right to send his letter. If Christians are concerned with the spiritual welfare of the people, they must be concerned with their material needs. The poor who are in a majority must be looked after, rather than the interests of the few rich catered for.

We should never forget the words of the Magnificat, which some regard as being more revolutionary than the 'Marseillaise', and as important a revolutionary document as the Communist Manifesto drawn up by Marx and Engels. As with the Communist Manifesto, I am afraid too many either mouth the words of the Magnificat without meaning them or ignore it altogether.

Christian principles and Labour policies

The early Christians had what today would be called slogans. For example: 'If anyone will not work, let him not eat'; and 'There is neither Jew nor Greek, there is neither slave nor free, there is neither male nor female.' Those are both quotations from the Letters of St Paul (2 Thess. 3.10 and Gal. 3.28). In another Letter he wrote: 'There is no question of relieving others at the cost of hardship to yourselves; it is a question of equality. At the moment your surplus meets their need but one day your need may be met from their surplus. The aim is equality' (2 Cor. 8.14 NEB).

These are clear socialistic principles. The socialist view is that things should be owned in common, especially that the means of production, distribution and exchange should be publicly owned – or, to use another term, socially owned, with democratic control and management. Francisco Nitti, who was Professor of Political Economy at the University of Naples in 1890 and who was an acclaimed Roman Catholic scholar, said in his book *Catholic Socialism* that 'according to St Jerome opulence is always the result of theft, if not committed by the actual possessor, then by his predecessors'.

Such a view is not different from that of subsequent socialist thinkers. What it calls for is a redistribution of wealth, so that the poor receive a fair share of the wealth they create. This is not really the case today, despite the fact that the existence of trade unions has helped considerably in ensuring that workers by hand or by brain are given a better deal than they used to obtain before trade unions were formed.

Common ownership – a Christian concept

With regard to public ownership, that in essence is a concept of the early Church. As it says in Acts 4.32, the members of the first Christian communities were 'of one heart and of one soul, neither said any of them that aught of the things which he possessed was his own, but they had all things common'. St Cyprian in *Of Works and Arms* wrote: 'When at the first beginnings of the Church the mind flourished with great virtues, when the soul of the believers burned with a glow of faith yet new, then they had all things common, they initiated the divine law, the equality of God the Father.' Clement of Alexandria taught that 'all things are common and not for the rich to appropriate an undue share. That expression, therefore, "I possess and possess in abundance, why should I not enjoy?" is suitable neither to man nor to society . . . God has given to us the liberty of use, but only so far as necessary, and he has determined the use should be in common.'

It is quite clear, therefore, that the concept of owning things in common is both Christian and socialist. Most religious orders in the Church are communistic or socialistic in practice. What property there is is collectively owned and not held individually, apart from small personal items. In supporting socialism and working for a socialist society, there is no contradiction between that and working for one's religious concepts.

The important question is: does one concern oneself with personal salvation or collective salvation? Over the years, Labour's socialist beliefs have meant that Christian concepts of looking after the interests of the majority have been put into practice. It was the Labour Government of 1924, (a minority government without real power) which created the 'Wheatley' Housing Act that was responsible for the building of half a million council houses for rent – houses which went to the poor and needy. John Wheatley was a Roman Catholic, and in Glasgow, before the First World War, he had created a Catholic socialist society. His action was not applauded by the hierarchy of the Church, but what it did was to prove that one could be a left-wing socialist and a Catholic at the same time.

Wheatley put his Catholic and socialist ideas into effect once he became a Labour Minister. He recognized the dire need for homes among working people, and because of his beliefs he went forward while in political office to do all he could for those in need. It is generally recognized that Wheatley was the best of all the Labour Ministers in the 1924 Government and that he achieved more positive results than any of the others.

George Lansbury, in his book *My Life*, says: 'I also helped form the Church Socialist League.' That was before the First World War. He says that the members were a mixed bunch and that 'at one time it looked as if we would become a formidable power in the Church'. The League 'stirred up the Church Congresses held at Swansea, Barrow-in-Furness, Leicester and elsewhere'.

He and his friends such as Wheatley were applying their Christian beliefs to everyday life, and because of that they felt compelled to take the side of the poor and to work and fight to change society.

Lansbury summed up my own personal views of religion when he wrote: 'In the matter of religion I cannot think of those who strive to worship God in some other way than I do as either inferior or superior to myself. Religion and all questions concerning the spirit are so very much a personal matter that nobody can truthfully settle these matters for other people.'

Lansbury was a religious person and felt that in working for socialism he was also putting into effect his religious beliefs. He was involved, deeply involved, in Poplarism and went to prison with other councillors because of his convictions. He was both a Guardian of the Poor and a local town and borough councillor.

He came up against Canon Barnett who was at St Jude's. Lansbury says: 'I yield to nobody in my respect for Canon Barnett and his wife, but I am more concerned than ever that their whole philosophy of life was all wrong. They never took sides on anything, not even about religion. Nobody except themselves could possibly understand what they believed about God and the Christian religion, and as to politics, Socialism, Toryism and Liberalism all were a sort of jumble – nobody was quite right, everybody was a little wrong.'

The point about Lansbury's remarks is that Christians are by no means all socialists, and they can be divided, like anyone else, on political issues. This is seen clearly in the House of Commons, and in any Local Authority. To me, however, if one really has Christian charity and compassion, then one must surely be on the side of the downtrodden, the poor and the oppressed. One cannot be above the battle. Lansbury placed money, property and privilege at a much lower level than concern for human life. The poor in Poplar needed help and Lansbury was determined to fight for decent treatment of the poor who were outside the workhouse: as he put it, 'Hang the rates!'

For their defence of the poor, their so-called 'breach of the law', Lansbury and his fellow councillors went to prison. They were persecuted for their beliefs as the early Christians were and as some Christians are today. Lansbury later became the Leader of the Labour Party; but he was a pacifist and he became the victim of those who felt he was not the sort of worldly moderate leader that Labour required.

His socialism, however, was genuine moral socialism and to the end he kept his faith.

Religious socialists, inspired as they are by Christ's teachings, by his 'subversiveness', do everything they can to end poverty, to create employment, to build houses for the poor, to ensure that the mass of the children of the poor are given good educational opportunities and that they have a sound National Health Service backed by a comprehensive welfare state.

Jesus gave bread and fish to the masses who needed food. That 'providing' is what socialists try to do. It should be carried out not as a charitable act but as a right. Those who work or wish to work, who rely on work to live, have a right to work for full maintenance. It is that idea which lies behind the welfare state; and it is what Wheatley and Lansbury were advocating. The Church cannot retreat into a safe haven. It cannot say 'it is nothing to do with us', or 'the poor are not our responsibility'. Christ did not say that and neither can Christians say it today. If they do, they are, in essence, denying the basic tenets of the Christian teaching.

The evils of racism

It is the same in relation to race, immigration and colonial freedom. When I went to Sunday School, I remember a picture that was set before us. It was a picture of Christ surrounded by children, with the caption 'Suffer little children to come unto me'. They were not just white children. They were of different colour and of different nationalities. We are all God's children, made in his own image; therefore it follows logically that racism in any form is evil and has to be combated.

In Liverpool, along Princes Road (the heart of Liverpool 8, and therefore in the centre of Liverpool's black quarter), there is the statue of a black Christ made by the Liverpool sculptor, Arthur Dooley, who is both a Catholic and a socialist. The Christ is symbolic of the wounding of the black people. They have been crucified over the years through exploitation by the white oppressors, the white oppressors being the outposts of capitalist imperialism. Whites took over and dominated Africa, Asia and Latin America, using black people as slaves or cheap labour and fully exploiting the mineral resources of those countries in the interests of the imperialists' home country. The truth of the matter is that even the workers in the imperialists' homeland, such as Britain, gained at the expense of the indigenous peoples who were being exploited. Unfortunately, at times, the Church was part of that imperialist system and many missionaries, although doing good deeds on a personal level, actually helped to extend and secure imperialist domination.

It is pleasing, therefore, to see that in South Africa today the Anglican Church in particular is playing a progressive role and that Archbishop Tutu and most of the Anglican priests are totally identified with majority black rule. They are against apartheid and support the struggle of the black people to secure their rights and freedom. It would be wrong for the Church to withdraw from that fight. Christian principles dictate that the Church must be on the side of the oppressed, especially where there is injustice and where oppression is built into the system; it therefore cannot shrink from giving support to those compelled against their will to involve themselves in armed struggle. It would be totally hypocritical for the Church to condemn those involved in armed struggle, those who are fighting for freedom, while chaplains are attached to the armed forces of the imperialist powers and while bishops say prayers for victors in wars.

There are Christians who argue that Christians at all times must be pacifists. There are socialists who also argue that. It is not a view that I hold, as I believe that in the struggle to build a new world, to create God's Kingdom, it may be necessary at times to use force to protect oneself from those who would seek to oppress us by the destruction of democracy and thereby stop the onward progressive march of history.

The agreement reached by the Roman Catholic Church with Hitler did not stop Roman Catholics from being persecuted by his organization, and it did not stop church-men involving themselves in the anti-Hitler struggle. Christians throughout the world at moments of crisis have been forced to take sides. They could either continue to support the powers-that-be, the ruling classes and the establishment, or they could come down on the side of the people – against oppression and for the creation of a new society.

Archbishop Romero was shot down in his own church in El Salvador for siding with the people. He was in the best Christian tradition. The Christian must be a revolutionary, but a revolutionary who is also a reformist. What is required is 'revolutionary reformism'. It is both a Christian and a socialist concept. Herbert McCabe OP, writing in *New Blackfriars*, November 1966, and quoted in Brian Wicker's *First the Political Kingdom*, put the position very clearly: 'For me there is a place for reform – within the context of revolution. For me there is even a place for violence – within the context of non-violence and forgiveness the only intrinsically revolutionary act. The programme of Christianity is to subvert the world . . .' 'The Christian response seems to me . . . complex: God so loved the world that he gave his only Son . . . not to condemn the world but that the world might be saved through him. But do not love the world . . . If any one loves the world, love for the Father is not in him, and if you were of the world the world would love its own; but you are not of the world . . . therefore the world hates you. The world here is not Nature or Creation or Man, it is the actual political and social structures within which Christianity is at work. The world's hatred is shown in police actions, in being thrown out of churches, in being stoned or shot down for the sake of law and order by men who think they are doing a service to God.'

The South African Government condones its apartheid régime in the name of Christianity, with most of the Government being members or supporters of the Dutch Reformed Church. Similarly, in Latin-American countries, many of the hierarchy of the Roman Catholic Church give their support to dictators and reactionary régimes. It would be easy, then, to suggest that Christianity is a religion that is on the side of reaction. Here in Britain the Establishment claims the Church of England, and the Tories in particular view the Church as an arm of their Party, at the same time saying that the role of the Church is not to become involved in politics. They equate the political status quo with being non-political. Politics, they say, comes only from those who seek political and social change.

Years ago, Basil Mathews wrote a book entitled *The Clash of Colour – a Study in the Problems of Race*, published by the Church Missionary Society. In it he outlined the oppressive exploitation that took place in the various colonies. He pointed out: 'It is from the soil of Africa and from the labouring hands of Africans that we take coffee on the breakfast table. We owe to the Africans an inexhaustible catalogue of necessities, the African oak and leather of our chairs; the rubber of the golfball, the bat handle, or the tennis ball, or the heels of our shoes or the tyres of our motor-cycle . . . the gold that is the basis of the currency that we use is mined by Kaffirs (for a seventh of the world's whole store of gold comes from Africa).'

Mathews had sympathy with the blacks. He was against racial prejudice, but he did not take his support as far as

69

many church people would today when, increasingly, Christians are not just sympathetic to but are part of the struggle itself. Mathews certainly understood the position, pointing out that Burghordt de Bois, the Negro writer and orator, wrote immediately after the First World War in his book *Darkwater and the Negro* that 'wild and awful as this shameful war was, it is nothing to compare with that fight for freedom which black, brown and yellow men must and will make unless their oppression and humiliation and insults at the hands of the White World cease. The Dark World is going to submit to its present treatment just as long as it must and not one moment longer.'

The 'subject peoples' have, since the Second World War, in most countries won their independence, but unfortunately they have not always won real democracy and freedom. That struggle continues. Christians must not ignore these struggles and must be on the side of those who want genuine freedom of speech, of publication, of worship, of political action, of elections, etc. At the same time they have to recognize that Western democratic forms of government cannot automatically be transferred to the African, Asian and Latin-American countries. Forms of democracy must be relevant to each country, to each continent. They must develop naturally out of the struggles of the peoples in these areas.

I have said that socialism and Christianity are, for me, synonymous, that the one complements the other; but of course that is not a view that others would necessarily accept. The view I support was firmly and clearly outlined in a book by Fr Bede Onuoha, published in 1965: *The Elements of African Socialism*. He wrote: 'When Europeans try to form a judgement on African reality they generally do so on the basis of some abstractions, some "ism" or "ocracy" such as Communism, Autocracy, Liberty, Democracy, etc. Understandable as such an attitude may be, no African can afford the luxury. For the responsible African there can be only one point of departure, namely that black skeleton of a man, hungry, half-naked, sick, frustrated, lying on a narrow wooden board beside an open fireplace, in his dingy hut of mud walls and thatched roof, with a low door, without a window, sharing the same room not only with his entire family but also with his animals.'

That type of scene was reminiscent of what had been the position of the poor peasantry in Ireland, in the last century, as well as in other parts of Europe.

The socialist and Christian must be opposed to racism in all its forms. It is anti-socialist and anti-Christian. In Britain, socialists who are Christian should be in the forefront of the struggle against racism. Many blacks and Asians may not be Christians, but that is irrelevant. What is important is the acceptance of the belief that we are all God's children and therefore each and every person has a right to live in peace, and not to be discriminated against. All should be equal in society. The colour of one's skin, and one's social background, should not matter. When churchmen such as Bishop Huddleston involve themselves in the anti-apartheid movement, taking a stand as he did in South Africa, they give a lead to Christians throughout the world. The Bishop showed that Christianity could be a living religion; and I believe that he acts in the true spirit of Christ, giving hope to millions of people who might otherwise be living in total despair.

Christian renewal

Christianity, like other movements, needs to go through periods of renewal. At no time should Christians or, for that matter, socialists, he tied to a particular organization. What they should support are the basic principles of the movement which from time to time have to be rescued, updated and renewed.

Christianity cannot only be concerned with the spiritual needs of the people. Material needs are also important, and the two cannot be divorced. The idea that man does not live by bread alone is correct, but to have a spiritual existence, one's basic material needs must be catered for. It is important, however, to get this idea right. Concerning oneself with material needs must not then lead into its opposite where money, commerce and individual greed take over from spiritual needs. We should never forget how Christ entered the Temple, a Temple full of moneylenders, bankers and debt collectors, as well as sellers of goods and bargainers, all in unseemly discussion and tumult. He burst in saying, 'Take these things hence! Make not my Father's house a house of merchandise.' He further shouted, 'My house shall be called a house of prayer. But ye have made it a den of thieves.'

Christ loved the oppressed, and loathed the oppressor. He loved the poor and humble, and despised the rich and haughty. His disciples were simple people – fishermen and other workers. His was a true people's movement, a movement for the poor, designed to change and improve things, a movement that would create a revolution through reform by creating God's Kingdom here on earth.

What is important today is that Christ's basic principles should be translated into everyday terms – that the struggle he conducted then should be continued today – and that must mean the creation of a better, more just, classless society based on collective ownership and collective actions for the benefit of all. That is why a Christian can be not only a socialist, but a militant one as well. In fighting to change the world, to build the new Jerusalem, the Christian can, in my view, achieve that only through the socialist movement.

The Christian response to poverty

Part of that immediate struggle is to help in the election of a government that will express, perhaps unconsciously, Christian principles, putting into effect positive policies that are in line with these principles. The Party which I consider can do that is the Labour Party. It cannot be an accident that the Report of the Archbishop of Canterbury's Commission on Urban Priority Areas, *Faith in the City*, was best received on Labour's benches in the House of Commons and was criticized, at times strongly, by some Conservatives. Some modern Tories are convinced that the Church of England today is a hotbed of Marxism, penetrated no doubt by the 'Militant Tendency'.

Actually, in many respects the Archbishop's Report goes further and is therefore better than the Labour Party document, *Homes for the Future*. It does not, for instance, advocate the sale of council houses but argues that more must be built.

The report in Chapter 3, 'Theological Priorities', is absolutely correct when it says in paragraph 3.3: 'In this country we are confronted by an acute form of relative poverty – officially recognized as "multiple deprivation" – that is particularly concentrated in the urban priority areas, and that is caused to a great extent by circumstances beyond the control of those who are affected by it. There is a clear Christian duty to respond to this situation and "remember the poor" in our urban priority areas.'

The report goes on to say: 'It is against the background of the excessive individualism of much Christian thinking in the nineteenth century that we must place Marx's perception that evil is to be found, not just in the human heart, but in the very structures of economic and social relationships. This perception is also found to a notable degree in the Old Testament [from which, in fact, Marx may have derived it] where there is explicit recognition of the inevitable tendency of the rich to get richer and the poor poorer unless some constraint is imposed to limit the freedom of individuals to profit without restraint from a market economy.'

The core of Christian teaching as I understand it is that wealth created by the working masses should be properly distributed among the people, especially among those who actually create the wealth.

Today, there is growing up in the Church (not just the

Roman Catholic Church) the movement for Liberation Theology. It is particularly strong in Latin America, but by no means is it confined to that part of the world.

The report *Faith in the City* says: 'To all of us, the example of Liberation Theology opens up the possibility that new priorities, as well as new methods, can restore to us a theology, that is truly relevant to the needs and aspirations of people today. Therefore we have to apply the new theology to the situation that exists in Britain today.'

That is a view with which I fully concur. It was that type of theology, well before its present-day advocacy, that John Wheatley preached and applied. It was that sort of theology that George Lansbury preached and put into practice. It is the sort of theology that was advocated by Conrad Noel, Fr Jack Putterill, John Groser and by those who support the Jubilee Group today. It was the type of theology put forward by those who wrote the Slant Manifesto in Britain. Camilo Torres, the Colombian priest, lived and died by that theology. Torres was a revolutionary priest who lived with the Colombian guerrillas and was eventually shot by government forces on 15 February 1966.

There are those who believe they are following Christ but who, without looking at the terrible social and economic conditions of the people of Colombia at that time and today, would condemn Torres.

The socialist in Britain, the member of the Labour Party, who accepts Christ, must surely give support to the practical proposals on housing, for example, which are contained in *Faith in the City*.

The report pointed out that housing policies could be carried out by councils, if (*a*) they had the political commitments, and (*b*) the necessary financial aid. For example, the report says: 'The walk-up blocks can be very successfully "capped" [i.e. the top two storeys removed] and turned into very attractive terraces, as we have seen in Liverpool.'

At the same time a criticism is made of pre-Labour

Council policy in Liverpool, in the comments: 'Where small-scale "hard to let" inner city estates have been converted for home ownership, the finished product has been impressive, as we saw in Liverpool. But the design and environmental improvement that have been thought necessary to attract owner-occupiers are the same as those desired by the tenants.' The report rightly goes on to say: 'The lesson of this kind of development is that if money is spent on upgrading and intensive staffing and people are allowed to occupy the space they feel they require rather than the space they are allocated, then the image of the housing is transformed. But had these features been incorporated originally, the estate might not have become "hard to let" in the first place.'

On page 250 of the report there is a section headed 'Public Housing: the Way Forward'. In paragraph 10.72 the report rightly says: 'The great importance of the public housing ideal was that it broke the link between poverty and living conditions. The poor did not have to live in poor housing. But this link is now being re-established . . . Net capital spending was cut by 44 per cent in volume terms between 1975/76 and 1979/80 and by 52 per cent in cash terms between 1979/80 and 1984/85. The result is that the number of new homes started in the public sector has dropped over the last decade from 174,000 in 1975 to 38,000 in 1984. At the same time there has been a shift in expenditure away from the metropolitan districts and London in favour of the shire districts.'

In the conclusion on the chapter on housing, the report says: 'What is beyond dispute we believe is that a continuing emphasis upon home ownership alone will not solve the housing problems of the urban priority areas.'

The report puts forward five main recommendations, all of which socialists can work for and support. It has had its effect on politicians inside and outside Parliament, and in my view is the way in which the Church should act. It should pressurize the politicians and call on those who are

Christians to support the type of policies advocated. I believe that kind of interference in politics is fully justified. It is in line with basic Christian teaching, and rightly shows its bias towards the poor, as the early Christian Fathers did.

Peace and disarmament

The same can be said of the Church of England's Report and the arguments about the atom bomb. Christians cannot be indifferent to the bomb. They cannot say 'it is nothing to do with us'. There are millions of Christians all over the world who are strongly opposed to the use and manufacture of atomic weapons. Christians from the very outset were involved in the creation of CND. Today they are among the women of Greenham Common. They picket missile bases, they carry out illegal acts by trespassing and cutting fences and cheerfully take their place among those who are sent to prison or are fined for their actions and beliefs.

Women should be allowed to play a full part in the Church and should be ordained. In my view that would be in line with the best traditions of the Christian religion. The men and women of the peace movement are putting into practice the basic tenets of the Church, and because of this they are attacked as 'loonies', 'subversives', 'egocentrics', 'idiots', etc. The same sort of charges were hurled at Christ in his time, for doing much the same thing.

The Anglican Report on nuclear weapons was not fully accepted at the General Synod. That was regrettable; but it did receive widespread support and the arguments put forward were, in my opinion, almost unanswerable.

The Labour Party is the only party which has a policy for getting rid of all nuclear weapons and bases from and around Britain's shores. To that extent, Labour's policy is a Christian one and, again, it cannot be an accident that the Church of England Report runs parallel to the ideas and policies of the Labour Party.

Also, it should not be forgotten that the Roman Catholic

bishops of the USA have made clear their opposition to nuclear weapons.

With regard to the Church of England's position, certainly of those who drew up the report *The Church and the Bomb*, published in 1982, I believe the moral argument against the bomb was more than convincingly put in that report.

In 1983 a report of the Alternative Defence Commission was issued, called *Defence without the Bomb*. The commission had been set up by the Lansbury House Trust Fund, and included a number of Christians. All members of the commission agreed that the main threats to Britain are from the two great powers, the Soviet Union and the USA. They argued that a Soviet invasion of Western Europe was unlikely, as they could not see any political or economic interests that would lead the Soviet Union to undertake an invasion. But they felt that the Soviet Union, like other powers, could be 'tempted to try to extend the area under its control if there appeared to be no obstacles'. They also argued: 'In some circumstances a non-nuclear Britain could also face pressure of various kinds from the United States.'

The position of the USA with regard to British defence policy is of the greatest importance. It cannot be shrugged off, and placatory remarks made to the US leaders will not, in my view, be sufficient. As far back as October 1980, Duncan Campbell, writing in the *New Statesman*, said: 'In Britain, the US forces have at least 21 air bases in use or reserved for them, 9 transportation terminals, 17 weapon dumps and stores, 7 nuclear weapons stores, 38 communication facilities, 10 intelligence bases and ... sonar surveillance sites. Of these the majority clearly contribute at least as much to strategic global "US only" options as to the options for defending Europe.' No doubt since that date the situation has changed, but not in its essentials. Britain is very much locked into US policy – not just with regard to Europe, but on a world scale. It should be remembered that it was from bases in Britain that US bombers flew, and dropped their bombs on Libya, killing and maiming innocent people. It is the USA which is supporting the Contras in Nicaragua, and it is the USA which is supporting vicious dictators against the democratic forces in various parts of the world.

That does not make us anti-American, because there are two Americas, one of which is as much against the US administration's policy as we are, and includes thousands of Christians opposed to Reaganism because they *are* Christians and see their opposition to his policy as part of their fight for 'God's Kingdom'. They are on the side of the oppressed, of the sick, the downtrodden and the humble.

Precisely because of the somewhat 'Rambo'-type attitudes of the Reagan administration, the dangers for Britain are great, due to the numbers of bases here. There is no doubt that the very presence of US bases and facilities in our country means we are in the front line of nuclear warfare if the so-called deterrent system fails, as I believe it can. It is for that reason that it is essential to call for all US bases to be removed and facilities withdrawn, not only nuclear ones. That, however, is not yet the view of the majority of the Labour Party Conference, nor is the proposal to get out of NATO. There are, however, many Christians and socialists who believe this is essential.

What the Labour Party has believed for a long time is the need for the ending of the Warsaw and NATO Pacts, to work for a nuclear-free Europe and the removal of all foreign troops, East and West, from European soil. The policy has not been repudiated formally and it continues to be Labour's objective. It is one that can be understood, accepted and worked for by Christians who believe in peace and say to each other, 'Peace be with you'. They should therefore join in the struggle to achieve world-wide peace by first repudiating and working against all nuclear weapons and bases.

Trade unions – the right to organize
Trade unions are often portrayed as groups of ruthless men

and women who are power-hungry, selfish and therefore anti-social. It is a false picture, designed to injure the unions and justify the anti-union legislation introduced by the Conservative Government.

Unions were created by workers as defensive organizations. They were originally groups of working men and women who, because of their employment conditions, were compelled to organize, to fight for a living wage, to ensure that working people had rights and justly regulated hours of work. They opposed the competition of worker against worker and acted collectively.

In Britain unions were formed largely by Christians of one denomination or another. It was the selfishness of the employer which they combated and because of that many of them were persecuted, imprisoned or sent abroad to penal colonies.

Each year at Tolpuddle a march and meeting are held to commemorate the Tolpuddle Martyrs. These were the men who formed an Agricultural Labourers' Union, and were imprisoned and transported. Their leader was George Lovelace, and both he and his brother were active Christians. In forming the union, in fighting for the rights of the workers, they believed they were pursuing a Christian act, carrying out the teachings of Christ.

George Lovelace was the seventh child of a large family. Joyce Marlow, in her book about the Tolpuddle Martyrs, writes that it was said of the Lovelace brothers: 'They had, by dint of study and application, become so qualified in mental capacity as to be enabled to give lectures in the neighbourhood to their fellow-labourers and had been received into the Wesleyan Conference as preachers.'

George, the Methodist preacher, was sentenced to seven years transportation. His response was to issue a poem, 'God is Our Guide'.

> God is our guide, from field, from wave,
> From plough, from anvil, and from loom;

We came, our country's rights to save,
And speak a tyrant factor's doom;
We raise the watchword liberty;
We will, we will, we will be free.

God is our guide! No swords we draw.
We kindle not war's battle fires.
By reason, union, justice, law,
We claim the birthright of our sires;
We raise the watchword, liberty,
We will, we will, we will be free!!!

These brave, Christian working men were imprisoned, and then sent to New South Wales. George Lovelace was ill in Dorchester Prison, so he did not go with his brother and friends. He went to Van Diemen's Land later, on the convict ship *William Metcalfe*.

He wrote to his wife: 'Be satisfied, my dear Betsy, on my account. Depend on it, it will work together for good and we shall yet rejoice together. I hope you will pay particular attention to the morals and spiritual interest of the children. Don't send me any money to distress yourself. I shall do well, for He who is the Lord of the winds and waves will be my support in life and death.'

It has often been said that the Labour Party in Britain owes more to Methodism than to Marxism. While that is clearly a one-sided picture of the movement, it is true that Methodism was very influential in certain parts of the country. The primitive Methodists in particular played a prominent role in the creation of trade unions in the north of England – in the Durham minefields, for example.

The book *Methodism and the Struggle of the Working Classes, 1850–1900*, by R. F. Wearmouth, gives details of Methodists who were active in the formation and membership of trade unions; also, their involvement in political activities.

It also has to be said that many of the established-church clergy were against trade unions. J. C. Cox and H. F. Cox in their book. *The Rise of the Farm Labourer* write: 'Pulpit after pulpit in Warwickshire, Kent and elsewhere, is re-echoing the dire warnings of the insidious evil that lurks almost in the very name of unions – speaking the other day in his diocesan City at an agricultural dinner, the Bishop of Peterborough indulged in an impassioned burst of needless rhetoric against those who are expressing practical sympathy with the oppressed labourer.'

Christians were thus against Christians. The question is, who were really speaking and acting in the true spirit of Christ? Those defending the rich – the landowners, the industrialists, the capitalists – or those ordinary working men and women who, holding Christian beliefs, were fighting on behalf of the poor and the downtrodden?

It is an old story, going back to the Peasants' Revolt of 1381, when John Ball, the so-called Hedge Priest, took the side of the peasants against the rich and was hanged for it.

The truth of the matter is, as Wearmouth says, that 'the struggle of the agricultural labourer had its counterpart in the struggle of the industrial worker. Both had to struggle hard and long against their masters for the right to combine, for the right to collective bargaining on wages, hours, conditions of work and for a decent standard of life.'

Part of that struggle has been to keep the Sabbath Day a non-working day for most workers, to ensure that shop-workers are not forced to work on Sundays. Despite that, voices were raised in government circles by some professed Christians who called for Sunday to be virtually a normal working day. Such a move was opposed by MPs who believed in the Christian Sunday and by trade unionists, MPs and others who were concerned to protect workers' rights and conditions.

During the nineteenth century the conditions of shop-workers were appalling. The arrangements for their living-in were meagre, to say the least. They were often required to work late in the shop, and sitting-rooms for them to use were deemed unnecessary. In many cases the only relaxation and social intercourse they had was in the local pubs.

Some shopkeepers who considered themselves good Christians seemed not to care about what happened to their staff on the Sabbath Day. An article published in the Church of England Magazine, and referred to by Wilfred B. Whittaker in his book *Victorian and Edwardian Shop Workers*, said: 'For those whose salaries are small, or worse still, for the "improvers" who have no salary, the Sunday is a dreadful problem . . . Some walk the streets, some sit in the parks. Some can be traced going from church to church to find one which is warmest, where they rest and doze through the time of service, before again setting out on their weary pilgrimage . . .

'In the places to which they resort to buy food, the acquaintances which they must make, and the snares into which they fall, are only the natural result of a state of things which is a disgrace to any Christian country.'

The conditions of the workforce were the direct result of the fierce competition between shop owners. The hours of opening were not restricted, and shops were often kept open only because the next-door neighbour's shop had not closed. At the same time, worker was set against worker, with some believing that because they were clerks, etc., they were superior to their fellow workers. The struggle to obtain proper regulation of hours, pay and conditions was long and hard. Improvements came only after strenuous efforts. An Early Closing Association was set up. The Rev. F. J. W. Hesley, rector of St Peter's, Walworth, said to the committee: 'I do not think the effect of this late shopping upon infant mortality has been sufficiently considered. Roughly speaking, a quarter of our babies die before they are a year old, and I believe it is very largely due to their being kept out so late at night, and being taken into public houses with all the accompanying smell and heat.'

The free-competition argument was, as could be expected, advanced against early closing. One woman, a Miss Nora Wynne of the Freedom of Labour Defence

Association, said that shops must be free to remain open or there would be no competition among them and prices would rise.

It is an argument we hear today from Tory politicians. Norman Tebbit, Chairman of the Conservative Party, has said that the Tories are the Party of Good Samaritans – that it is the duty of the individual, not of the DHSS, to help the poor. That would be fine if the rich individuals really did help. The truth is that they are usually compelled to help the weak, sick and helpless only because the state taxes them to do so. Therefore, we all become Good Samaritans, through the use of state money. It is not a question of handouts, it is a question of the state's accepting its responsibilities for us all. The DHSS is, therefore, the super-Good Samaritan, and that is a Christian concept. In the days of the Good Samaritan there was no DHSS.

I have given above an example of how competition led to long hours of work, bad conditions of employment, child deaths, disease, etc., all of which is the opposite to the type of society that Christ wished to create. Today the gains made by those workers are now at risk, for we know that Mrs Thatcher is in favour of 'Victorian' values, and the cry for Sunday trading has again been raised by those who are more concerned with profit than the well-being of the shopworkers. Should such legislation be introduced, it would mean the end of the British Sunday for which earlier generations fought so long and hard.

Conclusions

What, then, are the Christian principles in British politics? Obviously, we do not want to create a theocratic political system. That has been tried before in various parts of the world, with disastrous results. In my view, it is the early Christian principles which should be applied to political struggle, and we should aim not for a specific 'Christian' society that would really be unChristian, but for a society that is just and classless, with co-operation in place of competition, where riches are abolished, and where all have true equality. Such a system must be free, democratic, pluralist and anti-capitalist – in fact, a socialist society.

To achieve this we need a government which will tackle the needs of the underprivileged and the poor. Such a government at present can only be a Labour government, which would be but the first step towards a really socialist, egalitarian society.

The right use of wealth and power

R. H. Tawney wrote, I believe correctly: 'Compromise is as impossible between the Church of Christ and the idolatry of wealth, which is the practical religion of capitalist societies, as it was between the Church and the State idolatry of the Roman Empire.'

Is it possible to serve both God and Mammon? It is a question that all those who profess Christianity must ask themselves. If those who really accept the teachings of Christ, who want to create a new world here on earth, are honest with themselves, they surely must accept that they cannot support the capitalist system, with its competition, individual selfishness, power for the few – a society in which privilege is inbuilt for the rich and powerful.

Either one accepts individual wealth at the expense of the many, or one does not. To work for society as a whole is surely more important than to acquire wealth and material gains for oneself. The objective of socialists is to uplift society as a whole, to end poverty, to end privilege, to ensure that all are properly housed and fed and have equality of opportunity.

Socialists believe that it is essential to work for peace, both internally and externally; to solve problems by peaceful discussion, not by resorting to violence to settle issues. It is true that to defend freedom and human rights, to defend democratic society and extend it, to stop dictators from taking over, it may be necessary to use force to protect society, and that is also in line with Christian concepts.

Everyone has a right to a job. 'He that doth not work, neither shall he eat' is not just a socialist idea; it is also a Christian one. Obviously, those who, because of misfortune – through illness, disability or enforced unemployment – cannot work, should be helped by society as a whole by right and not by charity.

Labour's objective is to create full employment and to get people back to work. This can be done by more investment in construction, by creating the superstructure needed for the cities and towns, building roads, railways, etc. But what is really required is the rebuilding of our manufacturing base. That will need a planned approach and the proper use of the nation's resources. At the 1986 Tory Party Conference, Peter Walker said that oil had been given by God to Britain for the nation's use. The problem is, the 'gift' has not been properly used. It has been frittered away, rather than used to create employment. It has been used to finance unemployment, thus helping to undermine the best traditions and characteristics of the British people.

Britain's oil, coal and other raw materials can only be used properly if they are owned by the people as a whole. They must be seen as national assets, not a way in which to make money for a comparative few. Whole industries have been and are being privatized, purely for the Thatcherite ideology that private capitalism, private enterprise is best. The point is that while some so-called profit-sharing, through a diffusion of share ownership, may take place immediately after privatization, it does not last. The shares are quickly bought out by the financial institutions and power is concentrated into fewer and fewer hands. Industrial and financial power is being directed increasingly into the hands of those who run the multinational companies. They who pay the piper call the tune. The multinationals exploit the peoples of the third world, and while in the advanced countries where the multinationals have their headquarters, workers who are fortunate enough to be employed receive relatively high pay and good conditions, in the third world the people face stark poverty, starvation and despair. Instead of the advanced countries – most of which in the Western world are supposedly Christian – getting together to help those of the third world, they put increasing burdens onto them, forcing them more and more into debt.

The Catholic Institute, dealing with the third world over the years, has issued a whole series of pamphlets and booklets which have chapter and verse of the exploitation taking place in the third world and at the same time explain the role that Christians can play in the fight to remove this exploitation.

Politics and the Churches

In this essay I have not gone deeply into questions such as prayer, the sacrament, forms of worship, the apostolic tradition, etc. I have not entered into arguments about any particular denomination, or raised in detail discussions about the Reformation, the schism between East and West, or the growth in Britain of the dissenting Churches. They are all part of the Christian historical tradition and in their own way they are all part of the changing political scene on both a world and British scale.

Here in Britain we do not have to vote for political parties linked with religious sects or Churches. For instance, we do not have a Christian Democratic Party. We do not have a CDU, as in Germany. We do not have political parties tied to a particular Church, such as the Roman Catholic Church or the Church of England. That is good. If it were otherwise it would be a backward step and would create more problems than enough.

I believe that the Church of England should be disestablished. It should not be a state Church and ought not to have any privileged position.

The Tories, of course, still try to perpetuate the myth that the Church of England is the Tory Party at prayer. There *was* some truth in that, but the image now is rather worn-out and today Church of England priests are more than likely to be attacked by Tories for being 'trendy lefties' who are helping to undermine the country. Such Tories continue to expect the Church automatically to take the side of the Establishment, to defend capitalism and private enterprise; and when some churchmen do not do so, it is then suggested that they are not really Christians, when in fact because they do not defend the Establishment, and instead support the poor and oppose government policy, pressing for better housing and for employment, they are really carrying out Christian ideals.

In his recent book, *Bias to the Poor*, Bishop Sheppard of Liverpool makes it absolutely clear that he takes the side of the poor and puts forward policies which are very little different from some of those advocated by the Labour Party. He is not afraid to argue that Christians should be political.

In his book *Essays on Christian Politics and Kindred Subjects* William Temple wrote: '. . . it is not possible to limit Christianity to the individual alone. Christianity appeared in the world as a society. It was not indeed a society with a finished constitution presenting what officers it should have, or what its specific aims should be.'

Since it began, Christianity has gone through considerable changes. There have been so many differences within its ranks that, to some extent, it is difficult to define accurately who is Christian and who is not.

Because of all these divisions, the growth of the different Churches, the rise and fall of the sects, the strong theological differences, etc., for the purpose of this book I have referred to Christians and Christianity as meaning all those who profess to be Christians. To some extent, the same could apply to all those who call themselves socialists. There are, of course, certain basic features, tenets, to which all subscribe, and within that context they can be classified as accepting the faith. The Church itself has not only gone through a number of evolutionary phases, at times it has become the opposite to that which it was originally intended to be. It began as the society of the poor, later was transformed into the religion of the state, then became all-powerful; and a powerful universal state within states was defined by those who wanted to get back to its original principles. During the Middle Ages, a feeling developed that Christianity should be the poor man's charter. That feeling became the chief contributory cause of the rise of all those movements, whether they were Catholic or sup-posedly heretical, Franciscan or Waldensian, which were in being from the thirteenth century onwards. In Britain, they were embodied in the ideas of Wycliffe and, in a practical way, in the Peasants' Revolt of 1381. Troelsch, who studied these movements, was led to describe the period of the later Middle Ages as the *Laiechristentum*, the time of the common man's Christianity. Political struggle and political involvement has been endemic in Christianity from the very beginning, and whether some like it or not, that is still the case today. The rise of Protestantism was part of the struggle for political freedom, for democracy, for the right to speak freely, which is now accepted by most Christians, no matter to which branch of the faith they belong.

As I have said throughout this essay, the Church has a number of currents within it, the basic concept being the creation of God's Kingdom on earth, the need to create a society where things are owned in common, and where people act together for the common weal. At the same time, individuals have rights, minds of their own, and they must be given every facility to use them. Yet they must not be allowed to put themselves above society, to be avaricious, to use wealth and power at the expense of the majority. The individual's rights must be part of the collective whole and those rights, together with the obligations, must be accepted by all.

This position is held by those who are Christian socialists

and who are Catholic. The rise of Anglo-Catholicism in the Church of England, which 'restored the mass to its true position' was understood to mean that the bread and wine of the Eucharist was the consecrating of the whole of life and not only the personal rescue of the individual.

The view put forward is that because Christianity is working for a new social order, which embodies service and sacrifice, the Holy Communion is the supreme act of that sacrifice, of service and fellowship. This sacrifice is accepted as part of present-day realities. The sacrificial meal is the collective acceptance of the new society being worked for and is, therefore, a new covenant, the embodiment of the common life that is being sought.

It is therefore no accident that Christian socialism is perhaps stronger among the clergy of the Anglo-Catholic wing of the Church of England than in certain other sections. Nevertheless, one does not have to be an Anglo-Catholic to accept that Christianity is the religion of the common man – that it is the poor that are blessed and should be supported. Christians of all denominations can and do adhere to socialist principles, precisely because they see the one as the extension of the other.

The spiritual needs of mankind

Those who believe this are therefore forced to be political. It could not be otherwise. Man is, in fact, the centre of Christianity. Christianity divorced from man becomes a mere fantasy religion, removed from reality; yet reality, i.e. the real world, is surely central to Christian concepts. It is about men and women and how society can be seen catering for the needs of the people, not just in a material sense, but also in a spiritual sense. Material needs, comfort, benefits, are what are preached by capitalism. No one denies that the capitalist system has not encouraged industrial growth and development. It has. It has created social production, yet has allowed that social production to be channelled into individual ownership, because the means of production, distribution and exchange have not been socially owned but owned by individuals or institutions acting on behalf of one section of society as against the interests of the majority.

Men's and women's needs can be met today because of the development of modern technology. Abundance is available to all, not just in the developed world, but also in the so-called third world. What is necessary is that society should be organized differently, i.e. to harness production to meet the needs of all the people and to ensure that poverty is wiped out, by providing a good Health Service which is free and by making certain that the elderly and the sick are looked after and integrated into society as a whole. Ageism, sexism, discrimination of all kinds must cease, and that means the acceptance of both Christian and socialist principles.

Future British society must be part of world society. It is impossible to put an iron curtain around our country, nor should we try. The European peoples have the opportunity to lead the way. They can unite as socialists to create a new society by building a socialist Europe based on the concepts of social ownership, democracy and freedom. Such a perspective is only a pipe-dream, however, if we are afraid. We must look to the future; and those who are Christians, wanting to build God's Kingdom, can play their part fully in this transformation of society. They can become political by joining the socialist movement. In Britain, that means supporting the Labour Party. I am pleased to say that in my local Party we have a Church of England priest and a Roman Catholic priest, as well as ministers of the Methodist Church and others. We also have those who reject religion, some of whom are Marxists of various hues. That is how it should be. There is a vital need to exchange ideas and fight together for the common good. I agree with C. E. Osborne, formerly Rector of Wallsend, who, in his book *Christian Ideas in Political History* ended by saying: 'Christianity and Man were made for each other. Man needs Christ's religion.

he cannot get on without it. It is therefore "still in its great morning".'

I believe Christians and non-Christians should work together to change the world. In doing so, they will be putting into practice Christ's teaching, even if most may not recognize it.

BIBLIOGRAPHY

Baker, A. E., *William Temple and his Message*. Pelican Books 1946.

Beer, Max, *A History of British Socialism*, vol. 1. George Allen & Unwin 1953.

Brown, W. H., *Charles Kingsley*. Fisher Unwin/The Co-operative Union 1924.

Church of England Report, *The Church and the Bomb*. Taylor & Francis 1982.

Church of England Report, *Faith in the City*. 1986.

Clifford, John, *Socialism and the Teaching of Christ*. Fabian Tract no. 78.

Gutierrez, Gustavo, *A Theology of Liberation*. SCM Press 1971.

Hardie, J. Keir, *From Serfdom to Socialism*. George Allen 1907.

Howse, E. Marshall, *Saints in Politics – The Clapham Sect*. George Allen & Unwin 1953.

Husslien, Joseph, *Bible and Labour*. Sands 1924.

Kautsky, Karl, *Foundations of Christianity*. New York, Russell 1953.

Kellett, E. F., *A Short History of Religion*. Gollancz 1957.

Klugman, J., ed., *Dialogue of Christianity and Marxism*. Lawrence & Wishart 1966.

Marlow, Joyce, *The Tolpuddle Martyrs*. André Deutsch 1972.

Mathews, Basil, *The Clash of Colour – a Study in the Problems of Race*. Church Missionary Society 1928.

Nitti, Francisco, *Catholic Socialism*. New York, Swan Sonnenschein 1895.

Noel, Conrad, *Jesus the Heretic*. The Religious Book Club 1940.

Noel, Conrad, *Autobiography*. Dent 1946.

Onuoha, Bede, *The Elements of African Socialism*. André Deutsch 1965.

Osborne, C. E., *Christian Ideas in Political History*. John Murray 1929.

Pease, E. R., *History of the Fabian Society*. Fifield 1916.

St John, John, *Religion and Social Justice*. Religious and Moral Education Press 1985.

Segundo, J. L., *The Liberation of Theology*. New York, Orbis Books 1982.

Sheppard, David, *Bias to the Poor*. Hodder & Stoughton 1983.

'Slant Manifesto' – Catholics and the Left. Sheed & Ward 1966.

Smyth, J. Patterson, *A People's Life of Christ*. Hodder & Stoughton 1926.

Sobrino, Jon, *Christology at the Crossroads – A Latin-American View*. SCM Press 1978.

Soper, Donald, *Church and Tower Hill*. Hodder & Stoughton 1934.

Tawney, R. H., *Religion and the Rise of Capitalism*. Pelican Books 1938.

Temple, William, *Essays in Christian Politics*. Longman, Green 1927.

Torres, Camilo, *Priest and Revolutionary*. Sheed & Ward 1968.

Trevelyan, G. M., *England in the Age of Wycliffe*. 2nd edn, Longman 1972.

Wearmouth, R. F., *Methodism and the Struggle of the Working Classes, 1850–1900*. Edgar Backus 1954.

Whittaker, W. B., *Victorian and Edwardian Shop Workers*. David & Charles 1973.

Part Three

The Case for the Liberal/SDP Alliance

ALAN BEITH

Christianity and political power

Throughout most of its history Christianity has found itself engaged in various ways with political power. It has not always been by choice: sometimes it has been the unwilling relationship of the persecuted to the persecutor. Sometimes it has been the subordination of an unwilling state apparatus to a powerful Church. Sometimes the state has sought to control the Church so as to ensure that it does not become a rival power base: it is a condition we associate with traditional established churches, including the Church of England at times in its history; equally, however, it describes much of the relationship between the Ministry of Religious Affairs and the leadership of the Russian Orthodox Church in the Soviet Union.

Sometimes the relationship between Churches and the state has been one of tension and hostility; sometimes of cosy co-operation or uncritical support.

There is a view current among prominent Conservatives that just such a cosy relationship should exist, in which the Church, and particularly the Church of England, should be supportive rather than critical of the state. It harks back to the Erastian concept of a church at the service of the state, and it finds vigorous expression whenever synods or bishops indulge themselves in observations on topics of the day. The General Synod vote on sanctions against South Africa was particularly productive of this sort of reaction, as was the report of the Archbishop of Canterbury's Commission entitled *Faith in the City*. Almost anything the Bishop of Durham says on topics of the day (not to mention his comments on theological issues) can expect the same response. One Tory MP's response to the *Faith in the City* report was to assert that the Church of England was now being run by 'a load of Communist clerics' (John Carlisle,

Daily Telegraph, 2 December 1985) while an unnamed Cabinet Minister is said to have called the same document 'pure Marxist theology'. Mr Robert Adley, MP, questioned whether bishops, 'although decorative in their purple robes' were 'any longer entitled to be taken seriously as political commentators with a built-in right to sit in the House of Lords'.

At this juncture it is not the argument about the political direction of the report which is significant, but the assumption of those who criticize it that its publication represented a kind of disloyalty to the state, or to Christian values, or to both. There is also in these reactions a suggestion of episcopal or synodical infallibility which is entirely foreign to the doctrines of the Church of England, and even more alien to the Dissenting tradition. There is no reason in either tradition to assume that the utterances of one individual or even of a committee represent a required Christian view. A bishop can be found to support almost any political proposition, and synods and committees are not noted for unfailing consistency.

Those who display these reactions are not, in practice, propounding the doctrine that the Church should be excluded from all involvement in the political process, but criticizing the direction which that involvement is currently taking. It is not the same as the view taken, for example, by some in groups such as the Exclusive Brethren who hold that the need to be 'apart' and not to be 'unequally yoked with unbelievers' requires the Christian to cut himself off entirely from the political world (although even these groups find themselves seeking representation in the secular courts or in the political process in defence of their interests over such issues as military service or the payment of rates on their meeting-houses); nor is it quite the same as the sophisticated analysis developed in his 1978 Reith lectures by Dr Edward Norman, who argues that modern Christians have allowed a particular set of political conclusions to supplant the eternal in their perception of Christianity, bringing about 'the internal transformation of the faith itself, so that it comes to be defined in terms of political values'. His account is thought-provoking but bears none of the stamp of Christ's compassion and love for humankind.

What, then, is the basis of Christian involvement in political life, and what political conclusions flow from it?

The fundamental biblical source for Christian involvement in politics, for many of us, lies in the teaching of Jesus about responsibility to others. 'When saw we thee an hungered, or athirst, or a stranger, or naked, or sick, or in prison, and did not minister unto thee? . . . Inasmuch as ye did it not to one of the least of these, ye did it not unto me.' The ministry of Jesus speaks by precept and example of the obligation to serve the needs of others. Experience teaches us that, although individual service remains central to Christian living, there are means now available to us of meeting need which require collective effort. By organizing into friendly societies people discovered that they could tide each other over times of adversity. By subscribing jointly to the establishment of infirmaries people found that they could treat illness more effectively. We have discovered that with resources on the scale available to the state it is possible to cure and treat illness to an extent not possible by individual or voluntary collective effort. We have identified areas of poverty so great that they defy the limited scope of individual good works. Questions remain about what should be the balance of public and private, of collective and individual, in meeting these needs, but the perception that they exist and that the state has some part to play in meeting them is fundamental to Christian involvement in politics.

There are, moreover, areas of need in which the activity of the state is not only vital but also potentially harmful. In seeking to feed the hungry we recognize the need for both individual and collective effort – we contribute to Oxfam, to Christian Aid or to Live Aid, yet we feel that the state needs to do more to back this support with further resources. We also discover, however, that in misguided policies pursued by governments of both rich and poor countries lies the risk of more hunger. We become involved in contending that the third world's scarce resources would be better spent on irrigation than on arms, and that lending policies which make poor countries net contributors to the wealth of rich countries are selfishness dressed up as charity.

We discover that much human misery is caused by violent crime, by the abuse of alcohol or by drugs, and we therefore look for ways in which the state can maintain the peace, restrain wrong, and prevent dangerous materials from being misused. We find that it rests with the state to decide whether the stranger, in the form of the refugee or the immigrant, is to be taken in, and we seek more compassion in such decisions.

There is another, related aspect of Christ's example: his indignant refusal to accept that evil should go unchallenged. He turned over the tables of the Temple moneylenders because their shady dealings despoiled the courts of God. He railed against the hypocrisy of the scribes and Pharisees. He told stories designed to throw into sharp relief the failures of spiritual leaders in the society of his day, and contrasted their attitude with the kindness of poor and outcast people. Anger at evil is a proper Christian sentiment, and has driven Christians into political action through many centuries. It was anger which drove Wilberforce on through the decades until the slave trade was abolished. It was a refusal to accept the continuance of a great evil that made Christian politicians fight for laws to bring children out of the mines. It was anger at a social evil which led Martin Luther King to devote his life to his dream of freedom. It is anger over the failure to recognize the status of human life created by God which makes arguments about abortion so intense. That anger is a proper part of the Christian response to evil, directed as it must be into constructive efforts for change.

There are other reasons known to history for the involvement of the Churches in politics. Sometimes their activity has been designed to use the power of the state as a means of advancing or maintaining a particular denominational view, to such an extent that the protection of Church and of state have seemed to be the same thing. In its most extreme form it has been the basis of martyrdom; in less extreme form it has meant the exclusion of dissenting religious groups from freedom of worship from office. It took a political battle to gain for English Nonconformists the right to go to university. Until the last century Catholics were kept out of Parliament by the requirement to take an oath so stringent that it not only involved condemning transubstantiation and the invocation of saints as idolatrous, but insisted that these things should be abjured 'in the plain and ordinary sense of the words ... as they are commonly understood by English Protestants without any evasion, equivocation, or mental reservation whatsoever'.

But at some time or other most Churches have had some sort of interest to pursue through their political involvement, and one which would widely be regarded as legitimate. A great deal of the political interest of the Roman Catholic Church in England has been focused on the maintenance of the facilities for state-supported Catholic education. Fifty years ago, much of the focus of Nonconformist politics was provided by the battle to free their children from the obligation to attend Church of England schools at which they were taught the church catechism.

The pursuit of church interests, however legitimate, must always be secondary to the objective of the Christian to serve others through political activity.

What form should Christian political activity take?

In some countries it has taken the form of a church party, and the suggestion that a Christian party should be formed still crops up in the occasional church meeting. Such a course will not work. No church or Christian party will ever embrace all Christians, and most of those which have existed have represented one wing of the Church rather than the whole Christian community. Even if the idea were still acceptable, it has the further shortcomings that it tends to emphasize the interests of the Church rather than its obligations and, even more important, it denies the possibility of diverse political choice and robs other political parties of Christian influence within political philosophies which are not incompatible with Christianity.

Some Churches and church leaders have, however, thought it appropriate to direct or guide the political choice of their members at a particular election. This has all the same disadvantages, and denies the right of individual judgement in Christian living. It is a practice sometimes associated with the Irish tradition of Roman Catholicism, notably in its emergence in some of the cities and in the USA, and with an earlier generation of Tory parsons in the Church of England. It is normally viewed with great hostility by Nonconformists, who cherish individual rights in particular, but ironically it is often they who have shown the strongest sectarian political identification (notably with the Liberal Party). The Bible Christians, a West Country Methodist sect of great local influence which later became part of the modern Methodist Church, passed at their 1905 Conference a resolution calling on the nation to 'shake itself free from the incubus of a government dominated by the priest and the publican'. It was, of course, a Tory government: the implication that West Country Bible Christians should vote Liberal hardly needed any further stress; and, so far as we know, they did.

The United States has witnessed the development and indeed the manipulation of an extreme version of the 'direction to vote' in the guise of the Moral Majority, a movement which, backed by all the apparatus of TV and computer mailing, seeks to deliver the votes of Christians not only for specific candidates but also for specific propositions. It has views on everything from the right of the citizen to carry arms (which it favours) to abortion (which it is against), and from school prayers (for) to the Panama

Canal Treaty (against). Some of the specific demands of the movement seem strikingly unChristian – for instance, its apparently unrestrained demand for the escalation of the arms race by the USA, but what is equally unacceptable to many Christians is the packaging of issues on the extraordinary basis that someone who is opposed on religious grounds to abortion must feel impelled by the same convictions to oppose the Panama Canal Treaty. Candidates for Congress who do not score well on this amazing mixed bag of issues do not rate as worthy of Moral Majority support.

It is notable that no equivalent movement has developed in Britain. There are, of course, groups campaigning on the same issues and on some similar groups of issues, but none has dared to suggest a Christian political prospectus so all-embracing and so specific. There is real doubt that any comparable constituency exists for a distinctly right-wing political prospectus among the range of religious backgrounds to which America's Moral Majority has successfully pitched its appeal. Evangelicals, Catholics and Nonconformists at whom such an appeal might be directed do not generally share the far-right presuppositions on which the movement is based.

Christian belief does not free the individual from political choice. Indeed, it is in the nature of Christ's teaching that it provides a basis for life but does not free us from the choices and the difficulties of living. People constantly came to Jesus to ask for precise answers to specific questions, and it was his way to leave them not with easy answers but with fresh questions. So the New Testament offers no blueprint for the political order, no guidance as to the precise role of the state, and no definition of such things as the proper extent of trade union power. It is, moreover, a matter of practical Christian experience capable of ready demonstration that people of unquestioned Christian commitment and piety can be found occupying numerous different points on the political spectrum, because they have drawn different conclusions about the application to politics of Christian principles. However, the lack of a clear biblical basis for political choice has not stopped Churches and church organizations from advocating specific programmes, just as they have sought to apply the gospel to other aspects of life.

But these pronouncements, equally, have not freed the individual from the exercise of his own judgement on matters of political choice. Even in the more authoritarian wings of Christian tradition, whether in traditional Catholicism or strict Protestant fundamentalism, enough different choices have been advanced over the years to leave the individual with no unambiguous political direction. In the more individualistic traditions such as British Nonconformity there is a certain suspicion of political direction supplied by the Church or its leaders, although this did not prevent a notably close identification between leading Nonconformists and Liberalism. The choice therefore remains. The application of Christian principles has led me to choose Liberalism, and to welcome the opportunity to further the objectives of Liberalism by working in alliance with the SDP. In this essay I seek to indicate why I have made that choice and why I have no hesitation in commending it to other Christians enthusiastically, but in doing so I cast no doubt on the commitment of Christians who draw different political conclusions from the same basic beliefs.

Can a Christian be a Conservative?
The question is often put within the Churches in terms which suggest that a decisive 'NO' is the anticipated answer. Experience dictates otherwise: there are clearly many genuine and committed Christians in the ranks of the Tory Party, whose religious commitment cannot be shown to be less than that of their fellow believers in the other parties. But it must be difficult at times. I can only give a personal answer as to why I never found it possible to square my religious beliefs with support for the Conservative Party, and why I do not recommend others to make the attempt.

The most compelling reason in the lifetime of the present government has been its lack of real Christian compassion, a lack which has been criticized by one wing of the Party itself. 'Inasmuch as ye did not unto these, ye did it not unto me' was what Jesus said about our failure to feed the hungry, to clothe the naked, to care for the sick and for those in prison. Yet we have had a government which has made a virtue of not doing these things, or at least doing less of them. Cuts in overseas aid, and the turning away of overseas students from poor countries provide very specific examples. Equally relevant, however, was the decision that as a matter of policy it should be accepted that unemployment should be allowed to rise as the means by which inflation was to be controlled, rather than reducing the unemployment impact of anti-inflation policy by using other forms of restraint. Moreover, there has been a whole school of Conservative thought which has implied that unemployment is to a large extent the fault of the individual, who should 'get on his bike' and find work. There has been an absence of commitment to sharing the resources of the community, and there has been a specific shift in the tax burden to relieve by large amounts those with the highest incomes, while increasing the burden of the lowest wage-earners.

There are some Conservatives who argue, in fact, that it is not the business of the state to show compassion: in doing so, they contend, the state would be usurping the role of the individual. Compassion exercised by the state on behalf of the individual, the argument runs, is not compassion at all: virtue under duress is not virtue at all. There are two obvious problems with this argument. For one thing, it leads to the conclusion that the state should do nothing of any positive value so as to leave the maximum scope for individual charity: it almost invites the state to create more problems so that individuals can display charity and compassion in solving them at an individual level. That is patently absurd. More importantly, it ignores the extent to which solutions are available to human problems which have defied solution at the individual level by the application of collective effort. Smallpox was conquered not by individual acts of compassion but by collective efforts in public health. Future famines may be relieved by individual charity, but they will not be prevented unless there is a collective effort to assist subsistence farming and to release some countries from intolerable international debt obligations.

A Christian employer can find a job for an extra individual, but a judicious programme of public sector investment could put hundreds of thousands back in work. The discovery that collective efforts through state and community activity can heal the sick, feed the hungry and improve the lot of millions should be embraced by Christians as a means of carrying further the commands of Christ. Such collective action is not without its difficulties, as can be seen when we examine the problems which arise in reconciling socialism and Christianity; and the New Testament provides no definition of the proper balance between individual and collective solutions to human misery. It must be clear, however, that for the state voluntarily to deny to its citizens a relief of misery which it is equipped to provide must be a denial of basic Christian commitment.

There is, on the other hand, a more traditional school of Conservatism which is less open to the charge that it eschews compassion and condemns collective effort. It is the school represented by those within the Conservative ranks who have opposed or criticized the Thatcherite philosophy and, as a result, have been designated 'wets'. (The very use of this pejorative term is an indication of the determination of the Thatcherites to get away from the idea of compassionate Conservatives: in a similar way they castigate 'do-gooders', thereby appearing to align themselves against the Son of Man who went about doing good.) The older school of Conservatism, however, was paternalistic, and saw no ideological barriers to the use of state power to accomplish social ends. It was the Conservatism of council-house building targets, of regional aid, and even of Rolls-Royce nationalization. It was in no sense egalitarian, and would be criticized by many for being no more than palliative in its good works, seeking only to reduce social tension and thereby sustain a society of inequality and privilege, but it left considerable scope for sincere compassion. Its practitioners believed that, within limits set by prudence, public opinion and the perception of the possible, it allowed the application of broad Christian principles to the activity of the state. It was the embodiment of what Betjeman called 'middle stump' C of E – Matins in a country church, with squire and parson in their proper places, benevolent if not bountiful to the peasantry, supportive of worthy causes.

To me, however, it remained hopelessly limited in its grasp of human misery, both in our own urban areas and in poor countries across the world. It was also tolerant, wittingly or unwittingly, of greed and speculation in human misery on an appalling scale. It was, indeed, the property speculation and Rachmanism tolerated by a Conservative government which fatally undermined it, cost it power and opened the way for ideological monetarism to replace this old Conservative philosophy. And it was a Conservative Prime Minister who so vividly described these things as the unacceptable face of capitalism.

But there was more than that which made the old Conservatism difficult to reconcile with my understanding of Christianity. It did not treat people as being of equal worth in the sight of God. Christ drew no distinction on the basis of race, social status, background or reputation. Yet the very essence of old-style Conservatism was the preservation of power in the hands of a limited circle of people, and the exclusion from that circle of all but a token representation of those who did not have the right background. It was, and still is in some parts of rural Britain, the party of the gentry. Having no ideology, its main political objective was to exclude from power the ideologies of which it disapproved – primarily socialism – and the people who did not conform to its view of the social order.

Abroad it was allied to or tolerant of those forces which denied basic human dignity, not only in Rhodesia and South Africa but also in many other colonies whose independence was delayed and whose leaders were imprisoned. The old-style Conservatives were slow to accept that apartheid in South Africa was a serious evil, and although there are some Conservatives who are as dedicated in their opposition to apartheid as most people on the political left, there are others even today whose expressed opposition to the doctrine seems more formal than real. It is striking that the Prime Minister seems to be able to work up much more indignation when she denounces sanctions as immoral than she has ever been known to do when expressing opposition to apartheid. Even more revealing was the fact that the 1985 Young Conservatives Conference passed a motion condemning apartheid (and doing no more than that) by 338 votes to 228. The discovery that so large a minority were not even prepared to come out against so evil a system speaks ill for the future of caring Conservatism.

Can a Christian be a socialist?
A question in that form would rarely be asked in many of the churches in this country. It might have been asked a century ago, when any threat to the existing social order was regarded in some circles as inevitably a threat to the Church. Indeed, the Marxist origins of theoretical socialism led to the presumption that it was an inherently atheistic philosophy, despite the fact that there were demonstrable Christian roots for many strands of British socialism. As Harold Wilson observed, the British Labour Movement owed more to Methodism than it did to Marx, and it owed quite a bit to other Christian traditions such as radical High Anglicanism and the conservative (with a small c) working-class Catholic communities of Clydeside and Lancashire.

Again, it is demonstrable from experience that in all these traditions were deeply committed Christians who espoused socialism, and there are still such people today.

Indeed, the question asked of Christians about socialism is often a quite different one – it is 'How can a Christian be anything other than a socialist?' It is, of course, a form of question sometimes asked by people who do not believe that the Labour Party is adequately socialist, and it is also a question imbued with the very arrogance which I have argued is so inappropriate to the Christian attempt to make political choices. It is based on the assumption that since Christ taught us to share what we have, to give away what we do not need, and to disregard our material needs, a justification is thereby provided for the creation of a state which does all these things for us.

As a doctrine it raises some fundamental problems. For one thing, it finds itself caught in a limbo between Marxism and democratic socialism. It must distinguish itself from Marxism because of the latter's atheistic features; but it challenges democratic and pragmatic versions of socialism because it has a built-in moral imperative. If it is the state's duty to share out wealth, which requires the confiscation and redistribution of excess wealth and income, and that duty is based on the same kind of moral imperative which the individual Christian seeks to obey, then the securing of majority support is no more than an expedient for the achievement of socialism. Stafford Cripps held something like that view. He argued that the Parliamentary machine was 'an instrument for the preservation of capitalism', and that a socialist government would need to be given 'absolute and unfettered power to pass comprehensive socialist measures with the utmost possible promptitude of dispatch';[1] G. D. H. Cole thought that the obstacles might be so great that a socialist government might have to 'make itself temporarily into a dictatorship'.[2] On such an analysis, it is the achievement of the Kingdom of God on earth through collectivist action which matters, not 'bourgeois democracy'.

Of course, many Christian socialists never accepted that implication. They fell instead into a different fallacy: that people would necessarily become better as they experienced a developing socialist society; people would appreciate the advantages and benefits of such a society, and problems of democratic consent would no longer arise. If there was a problem, it was transitional. The discovery that crime does not disappear as material standards improve and that the rich do not generally develop an enthusiasm for generosity exacted through the tax system has been an understandably disillusioning experience for many Christian socialists.

But it is, perhaps, unfair to dwell on Christian socialism when the real choice faced by Christians in Britain sympathetic to its philosophy has been whether or not to support the Labour Party. That peculiarly British institution is a complex of many different traditions, with a rapidly shifting balance of power, which has brought about drastic changes to it in the last few years. Certain features, however, have consistently put off many Christians from seeing it as a natural political expression of their beliefs.

For one thing, it draws from the Marxist section of its bookshelf a tendency to treat people not as individuals but as members of a class. Helpful though this may at times have been to the recognition that whole categories of people were oppressed by the same evils or in need of the same kind of material help, it is fundamentally destructive of that recognition of the individual which characterized Christ's dealings with people. If your interests are subsumed into those of a class, some higher authority can determine what they are: only if you are seen as an individual do you decide your interests for yourself. To anyone from a working-class background there are few things more galling than being told what is good for you by persons of privileged background whose understanding of your aspirations is necessarily dimmed by the fact that they have never had to do without any of the things you might want. Being lectured by Mr Wedgwood Benn about the need to share wealth, or by a socialist product of one of the most expensive public schools about priorities for comprehensive education, is not a pleasing prospect for any working-class individualist.

Secondly, the British Labour Party is so closely tied to the trade union movement that it has tended to lose the ability to develop a perception of the interests of the community as a whole. Christians have played a major part in the trade union movement from the very beginning, and still do so; the movement has been a major contributor to the fight for better working conditions. It has notable moments of altruism, when great leaders challenge their members to look beyond their own short-term interests. But it is also, by nature, a vehicle for the pressing of sectional interests. It is trade unionists who make absolutely certain that egalitarianism does not break out in the form of equality of wages: they fight for their members' differentials, and for the right to be better paid than someone else. And the Labour Party, with its conference and candidate-selection procedures largely controlled by the trade unions, takes its cue from them. It denounces incomes policies which are designed to ensure that the prosperity is shared, that inequality of incomes is narrowed and that one man's wage increase does not become a poorer man's price increase: it does so because of its commitment to the trade unions whose freedom of action is circumscribed by such policies. It supports closed shops and the exclusion from work of people who have not secured membership of a particular trade union; it connives at the coercion of workers who do not choose trade union membership or who feel in conscience unable to support a strike which will harm a vulnerable group in the community. None of this seems very Christian.

But perhaps the most compelling argument against Christian commitment to the Labour Party is that so many of its solutions seem likely to fail. They place excessive faith in the capacity of the state. Not only does the New

Testament give us no indication that state power is the preferred way to deal with the promotion of good and the battle against evil: experience strongly suggests that the state is particularly bad at some of these things. Very little in our experience of nationalized industry would lead one to suppose that more good would be done if the state assumed control of more of industry. Promises of large increases in pensions and benefits, together with other massive commitments to expenditure and worthy objectives look extremely unlikely to be realized by a party which, even if its sums add up more convincingly that they appear to, has an approach to the economy which will not produce the confidence or enterprise necessary to provide the means for these plans.

The two-party system

Both parties share one set of attitudes which is difficult to reconcile with Christianity. Observe the two-party shouting match across the floor of the House of Commons and you will find very little evidence of Christian humility. Each party has a marked tendency to belittle the work of the other, and sets as its prime objective the destruction of much of what the other has built.

Since the war Britain has suffered from successive governments overturning large parts of the legislation of their predecessors: there has been no sense that one party is willing to recognize and build on the achievements of the other, and no sense that a party would wish to seek broad support and consensus around its major reforms so that they would be capable of lasting through subsequent administrations of a different party. This is in large part a product of the electoral system, discussed later, but it also betrays a distinct lack of Christian humility and a distinct failure to see the good which is in others. Christ's ministry is full of instances in which he sought out the good in those whom the people of his own community regarded as outcasts, publicly recognizing their qualities.

In current politics, lack of respect for others has

developed into an alarming retreat from pluralism. In many local authorities which it controls, the Labour Party has sought to exclude all other parties from committees and to deny them the information they need in order to do their job as elected representatives. In some areas Labour councils have excluded voluntary organizations from participation in tackling social problems; in others they have used their grant-making powers to channel funds towards those organizations of which they approve and within which they exercise political control. They have banned newspapers from public libraries with their excuse that this is a way of condemning Mr Rupert Murdoch's activities as a proprietor, showing no regard to the way in which such a policy could be used against them by their opponents.

The Conservative response to this retreat from pluralism has been to join it. Instead of confining themselves to strengthening the basic democratic framework and the values by which it operates, they have used the actions of Labour councils as an excuse to destroy most of the independent power of local government, and in the case of the GLC as an excuse to abolish it altogether. They have themselves also exercised powers of appointment in both local and central government in a ruthless filling of places with Conservative supporters. They have seemed at times to be carrying out the promise of Canadian Conservative Leader Brian Mulroney that he would 'never appoint a Liberal to a job so long as there was a living, breathing Conservative left', when they should have been using their power to appoint the best people for the job, without regard to their political affiliation or whether they had any involvement in politics at all.

Common prudence might have suggested to both the Conservative Party and the Labour Party that, since they are likely to spend a considerable amount of their time in opposition either at national or at local government level, it would stand them in good stead to have safeguarded the values by which plural democracy operates. To any

Christian and any serious democrat there is an even more compelling argument that the values of pluralism must be maintained because other people are sometimes right, and it is the opening up of one's views to challenge which enables assertions to be tested, common ground established and sensible choices made.

Christianity and the Alliance

The Alliance of the Liberal Party and the SDP brought together two great reforming traditions in British politics. The values of Liberalism were deeply rooted in Christian traditions which sustained and motivated Gladstone throughout his long and productive leadership of party and country and from which Lloyd George drew all his inspiration. Those who founded the SDP came mainly from the democratic reforming wing of the British Labour Party, whose increasingly extreme stance they rejected: by forming a new party they attracted the support not only of others who shared their disillusionment with the Labour Party, but also from Thatcherite Conservatism and, in far larger numbers, people who had never belonged to a political party in their lives. What brought the parties together was the discovery that they agreed about so many of the solutions necessary for the nation's problems and the values on which those solutions were based, and that there would be no point at all in putting at risk the achievement of shared objectives by campaigning against each other.

In looking at the values of the Alliance and their relationship to Christian belief it is worth noting that the very creation of the Alliance depends on that humility and willingness to learn from others which is at the heart of the gospel. Humility is not a prized virtue in politics: it is generally thought weakening to a politician to recognize, at any rate in advance of an election, that parties other than his own have at least as good a chance of being right, and that he could usefully learn from them and perhaps work with them. Willingness to accept and do such things character-ized the formation of the Alliance, and continues in our recognition that we should be ready to work with any or all of the other parties for the common good if the parliament-ary situation calls for such co-operation. Labour and Conservative leaders continue to talk as if such co-operation is the ultimate betrayal, conveniently ignoring that they are extensively involved in coalitions – even coalitions with each other – in local government. To them, co-operation is an evil, justified only as a means to the end of securing political power which would otherwise be denied them.

It has also been crucial to the development of the Alliance that politicians should not merely be able to work with each other but to learn from each other and to profit by their own previous experience. It is a curious axiom of political life, at least in the British House of Commons, that politicians should at all costs avoid admitting that they have ever changed their minds. Such is the odium reserved for the politician who has learned from experience that it is more comfortable to persist in error than to imply fallibility by admitting to a change of mind. Some members of the SDP are castigated for espousing proportional representation when they did not do so for the whole of their earlier political life; so great is the desire of Ministers, including the Prime Minister, not to be caught out with evidence of changed views that civil servants solemnly deploy their famed drafting skills on prose which can make two irreconcilable views appear to be no more than gently differing shades of the same argument. There is no good reason for the process of learning by experience and by argument to be so despised as it is in British politics. The New Testament certainly calls for a different approach, with its constant illustration of the good which is to be found in others, and its promise that the Holy Spirit will guide us into new truth.

Many of the values characteristic of Liberalism and the Alliance appeal directly to Christian thinking. For example, there is the drawing together of individualism with recognition of the need for collective effort to tackle serious problems. While the modern-day Tory attacks collectivism and cuts back even the beneficial aspects of the work of the state, the Alliance recognizes that private health care and private education simply cannot meet the needs of the vast majority of people; but while the socialist extends the state's empire in the belief that its beneficent purpose justifies unlimited enlargement, the Liberal fights for the individual's right to choose.

There is a very striking biblical basis for seeking to keep these two requirements in balance. Jesus went about meeting need and never turned aside from those who were in need. When he gave us the example of the Good Samaritan he ridiculed all the excuses we put up for not responding to need when we find it. At the same time, however, he addressed people as individuals, and frequently urged them to help themselves as part of the process by which he would help them. He told the sick man to pick up his own bed and walk; he asked the man waiting by the pool whether he really wanted to be healed, before healing him. A society in which the individual plays no part in solving his own problems would not be recognizable as following Christ's own example.

It is a principle of Liberalism that the state is there to help the individual lead his own life and to maximize his freedom to choose that life for himself. Collective solutions may be the only means of tackling some human problems, but their use must be recognized as posing a potential threat to individual freedom: we should constantly be striving to protect the individual from the dominance of state or other collective organizations, and it is part of our philosophy to increase the individual's ability to take decisions about his own life. The Alliance seeks to enhance personal freedom and responsibility, to enable and equip the citizen to exercise power and responsibility, to provide a framework of social justice and to generate a sense of community.

Jesus treated people as individuals of equal worth, without any regard to their social status, their race, their occupation, or whether they were men or women (in a society which was notably restrictive of women). It is thus that we learn more about God's unqualified care for each individual; and it is thus that we are reminded of our obligations to all people. Jesus invited into his company those whom others would have excluded because of their nationality, their reputation, their low social status, their collaboration with an occupying power, or their previous activities. He declined to treat people merely as members of a class or group. Liberal determination to fight racism, discrimination against women, the persecution of minorities, all find a basis in Christ's example. That same example refuses to countenance the subordination of individual needs to those of group, race or class.

Jesus emphasized, however, our responsibilities to others, and any Christian model for the political and social order must surely seek to promote that sense of responsibility of each of us for our fellow human beings, whether in this country or overseas. The Alliance seeks to challenge society to a better and more dynamic vision than that implied by the assumption that the state simply holds the ring while a contest between unrestrained and powerful forces is waged in the name of the market economy, or the assumption that we can leave it to the state to make all things work together for good.

The Alliance is helped in its wish to speak for the common good – though not in funding its campaigns – by the fact that it is not tied to the vested interests of business or unions, and enjoys voting support from all sections and social groups in society. The identification of the other parties with the interests of labour on the one hand and capital on the other has weakened the ability of successive governments to unite the nation. It is an identification which has been heavily reinforced by the electoral system, and underpinned by the dominance of business in the financing of the Conservative Party and the trade unions in the financing of the Labour Party. The Alliance is able, at least at this stage in its history, to stand back from this conflict and recognize its dangers, particularly in the way in which it makes the House of Commons reflect and reinforce the battle-lines of industrial confrontation.

That is not to imply that the Alliance enjoys some permanent immunity from the forces which have identified parties closely with sectional interests: it is simply that the Alliance in both its policy proposals and its base of support is currently able to challenge sectional interest, has an explicit commitment to do so and is uniquely well placed to do so. Without substantial Alliance gains in a General Election there will be no fundamental change in the direction of common purpose and away from sectionalism in British politics. The success of the Alliance is the key to that kind of change.

The making of Alliance policies

Even if Christians can express their faith through some of the values upheld by their chosen party, what happens when they have to come to terms with the party programme, let alone the trials and tribulations of government? The manifesto of any party is a compromise between various factions, wings, competing priorities, and differing assessments of what will command electoral support. Some of those with whom the compromises are made will not share the same priorities as the committed Christian, and other committed Christians will have sharply differing views about where the party's effort should be directed. In the case of the Liberal/SDP Alliance there is the further complication that the joint programme must be a compromise between the declared policies of two separate parties, each with its own distinct policy-making machinery. In reality the span of opinion within the Alliance is much narrower than the range represented within either of the other two parties: the Alliance does not have to bridge a gap as wide as that between Mr Benn and Mr Healey, or as profound as that between Mr Heath and Mrs Thatcher. But the public desire to see an Alliance which is more united than the other parties places a high premium on compromise and agreement.

All democratic politics involves compromise and accommodation. It is a process by which individuals band together to achieve as many of their cherished aims as they can persuade others to support. Politics without compromise has to be either dictatorship or the paralysis of government. The Christian can hardly want either of these stark alternatives. The path of Christian political action therefore leads not along some quiet byway but along the heavily-trafficked highway of political argument; it is a route which I travel in reasonable confidence that the Alliance vehicle is going in the same direction as a Christian ought to be going. I shall seek to set out why I believe that to be so.

A free society

The theme of freedom shines out from the pages of the Old Testament and the New. Moses led an oppressed people to a new freedom, and kings and prophets contended with the challenges and dangers which were faced. Jesus told an oppressed people that he had come to give them a spiritual freedom greater even than the earthly freedom they were denied; in doing so, he gave clear recognition to freedom as one of the most basic and justified aspirations of the human spirit.

The Liberal Party, as its constitution states, 'sets freedom first'. The SDP grew out of rebellion against a new authoritarianism in the Labour Party, and against policies which failed to defend basic freedoms. Maintaining and enhancing freedom is at the heart of Alliance policies. Individual freedom needs protecting against abuse both by the state and by powerful groups through the enactment of a

Bill of Rights, and the Alliance has consistently supported the incorporation of the European Convention on Human Rights into British domestic law. Similarly, we support Freedom of Information legislation designed to make government more open. We wish to strengthen and extend the machinery which protects groups which suffer discrimination, and to enable women to take their full place in all spheres of life.

Fundamental to the safeguarding of freedom, and one of the highest priorities of the Alliance, is the reform of the electoral system. Our present voting system grotesquely distorts the decisions of the electorate; not only does it underrepresent minorities by giving a quarter of the voters only one twenty-eighth of the seats: it gives to another minority the power of a majority. Mrs Thatcher's government gained what appeared to be a landslide victory at the last election, increasing its majority from 43 to 144, whereas its public support actually declined from 44 per cent of those who voted to 42 per cent, each of which is a minority. Policies which had been rejected by the majority were then pursued with redoubled vigour on the argument that a new and greater mandate had been given by the voters, which was certainly not so.

This endowing of class-based minorities with majority power has led to constant and damaging reversals of national policy on such major issues as nationalization and industrial relations, and it has discouraged governments from seeking wider support for measures which could, because of that wider support, last longer. Strong government does not rest in the ability to add numerous controversial pages to the Statute Book: the strongest government is one which can win popular consent for measures which will outlast it. It was notable that the wartime coalition produced measures which lasted for decades. Despite the significant support for electoral reform which exists within both the Conservative Party and the Labour Party, the leadership of each of them has resisted it resolutely, preferring the prospect of occasional total power followed by the repeal of their measures to the prospect of building a system in which they will be fairly represented and through which their achievements might be longer lasting.

The Alliance advocates an electoral system which not only removes the gross distortions of the present system, but also gives to individuals and minority groups a wider opportunity to influence the shape of Parliament. STV, the system used in many other countries and in trade union elections as well as elections to the General Synod of the Church of England, allows the voter to rank preferences; consequently it gives the voter the opportunity to choose between the various wings of the party. It also enables the voter to depart from preferred party allegiance in order to support a particular candidate, while ensuring that support is returned to other candidates of the preferred party if the other candidate does not need it. The system undoubtedly provides a means of increasing the voter's sense of involvement in the election, and would help to break down the sense of hopelessness which leads to low participation in many areas because voters of the various parties are unrepresented in large sections of the country.

Electoral reform would make it more likely, but not certain, that no party would have an overall majority and therefore that parties would have to work together in government. If the voters preferred otherwise and voted in a majority for a particular party, then that party would be able to gain an overall parliamentary majority. But if there is no majority, then it is right and potentially very productive that the support of more than one party should be brought together in order to build one. It offers the prospect of more broadly-based government, which would be welcome to anyone anxious to secure the unity of the country.

Freedom from fear
For many citizens the greatest perceived threat to freedom

comes not from the abuse of state power or the monopoly power of business or unions, but from violence and crime. An elderly person's fear of going out at night or a woman's fear of walking alone in lonely places illustrate just as significant a threat to freedom as the denial of a passport. The physical intimidation of a worker who does not wish to join a strike is as much as threat to civil liberty as the denial of the right to strike by the state. The rule of law is of fundamental importance to the securing of liberty, and those who enforce the law are crucial to the task of maintaining freedom. The Alliance therefore attaches particular importance to support for the police and to ensuring that the police retain the confidence of the community. We strongly oppose the idea of a national police force, and we want to strengthen liaison between police and all sections of the community. We want to see more community policing in villages and neighbourhood, and a major effort on crime-prevention measures in which people are encouraged to be good neighbours – a neighbourhood-watch scheme.

One of the most difficult areas for the application of Christian judgement is the punishment of crime, and the Christian commitment to forgiveness is often at variance with society's demand for retribution or revenge. The Conservative Government came into office with a belief, widely shared among the public at large, that 'tough' measures would reverse the rising trend in crime. Nothing of the kind has happened. The attempt to switch emphasis from rehabilitation to a 'short sharp shock' in the treatment of young offenders has been acknowledged on all sides to have been a failure. Crime rates have risen even faster while the Conservatives have been in office and while they have sought to apply a more retributive approach to punishment. Longer sentences have brought overcrowded jails which, for many, are the university of crime. It is obvious that no party has a ready answer to the problem, but we would place increasing emphasis on finding alternatives to prison for those offenders who can be made to realize the damage their crime has done to others and see the need to repay society by doing something useful.

When Christ forgave wrongdoers, they had first recognized their wrongdoing: a Christian penal system should be compassionate, but it must also be the means of indicating to the offender and to others the nature of their crime and the harm that it has done. Of course, some offenders represent such a potential danger to society that they must be imprisoned for the protection of others for very long periods, in some cases for the rest of their lives. We must also tackle those things which tend to increase crime, including deprivation, urban decay, and the alienation of whole groups from society, as well as the evils of drug and alcohol abuse.

Responsibility and power
Freedom demands responsibility; the Alliance believes that people will be more responsible if they are entrusted with more power. The Christian gospel is based on the same principle: God gives men and women the power to make a free choice. In policy terms it means that we seek to distribute power as widely as possible, to have it exercised at the lowest practicable level, and to give individuals as much of a say as is possible in the things which affect their lives.

In the political sphere, this means that we seek power for tenants in the running of the housing schemes in which they live, power for local communities through stronger local government, and democratic control of the power exercised over the nations and regions that make up the United Kingdom. It is the practice of both Conservatism and socialism to centralize power, so that it can be used in pursuit of nationally-determined policies; we seek to reverse that trend, which has been extraordinarily strong under Mrs Thatcher. During her period of office, local councils have been stripped of most of their power, particularly by the establishment of almost total central control over their spending, on the false assumption that Whitehall knows better than local people what a locality needs. Electoral reform in local government and more power for parish and neighbourhood councils could have overcome the authoritarian trends which the Labour left brought to local government, without destroying the system.

We see the same need to give people responsibility in the industrial as well as the political sphere. We wish to develop systems in which the worker has a share in the decisions of the enterprise in which he works and, through profit-sharing or share ownership, a stake in its success. The concept of partnership ought to be replacing that of two sides of industry with conflicting interests.

Caring about unemployment

Any government influenced by Christian values ought to regard the unemployment problem as one of its highest priorities for action. In the first place, as the report *Faith in the City* points out, it is a major cause of poverty in Britain. Secondly, it is a waste of resources. Thirdly, it leads people to believe that the community has no use for them and that they have no contribution to make to it. All parties are concerned about it, and none even pretends to have a policy capable of wholly overcoming the massive problem which has arisen over the last decade. The Conservative Government has, however, consciously chosen to accept higher levels of unemployment than would otherwise have arisen because it insisted that the only way to defeat inflation, which also has very damaging consequences for many sections of society, was to restrict public spending and investment very severely. The Labour Party has argued for much larger public spending, with the virtual certainty that further inflation would result from it.

What has distinguished the Alliance's approach has been the willingness to accept incomes policy as a component of its economic policy. With voluntary restraint as the first step we would also take reserve powers for a counter-inflation tax designed to discourage inflationary pay increases. This would give us greater freedom to stimulate the economy by a carefully costed programme of investment in the basic framework of facilities on which society and industry depend: transport, homes, hospitals, schools and the environment. Incomes policy would also allow a fairer share of sacrifice between private and public sectors, replacing the discriminatory and unfair restriction of public service pay, particularly among the lowest paid, which we have seen during the last few years.

The scope for success in such policies has, sadly, been reduced by the squandering of oil resources on short-term balancing of the budget, just as asset sales have been used to pay current bills rather than generate new public investment, but the attempt must still be made. Policies will also have to be pursued which help to reduce the gap between the prosperous South and the less prosperous regions of Britain, and which give encouragement to small business and self-employment. More successful and competitive manufacturing industry is essential to tackling unemployment, but service industries and small-scale activity will have an increasingly important part to play. Employment opportunities could be widened through job-sharing and more flexible retirement, and society needs to demonstrate that holding down a full-time job is not the only route to respect and fulfilment.

Prepared for life

Over the centuries the Churches have been deeply involved in education, recognizing its importance as the preparation for life. The Alliance shares that commitment to education, and believes that the provision of free education for all to the highest standards is one of the first responsibilities of government, whether national or local. We would protect the right of those who wished to do so to opt out of the state system at their own expense, but we do not wish to see people driven into private education by inadequacies in the state system. We recognize also the role which the Churches play within maintained education, and the particular benefits this partnership now brings. Church schools were once a source of intense controversy in which the Liberal Party was deeply involved, but it is notable that Christian parents from denominations which used to be hostile to each other now cross denominational boundaries in order to obtain a Christian-based education within the state-funded system.

Education and training have become competing activities: they should be brought together under a single ministry. We should accept the fact that education is a lifelong process, and make it easier for people to return to the system at later stages of life. Schools need to be equipped and staffed to achieve high standards and to give pupils the ability and the confidence to make the most of the opportunities which will come their way and to make well-informed choices about how they live. Access to further and higher education needs to be easier, especially for those groups in society who are consistently under-represented in our colleges. A loan system would have the opposite effect, so we wish to maintain the grant system and attempt to restore its value.

'Remember the poor' (Galatians 2.10)

The effect of the tax and benefit policies pursued by the Conservative Government has been to increase the gap between rich and poor. Tax reliefs, in particular, have been of great benefit to the highest earners, while the poorest continue to pay a high proportion of their income in tax or suffer from restrictions on benefit. Reductions in the standard rate of income tax continue this trend, but the Government has pressed them as a primary objective, and the Labour Party did not oppose the 1986 cut of 1p when the Alliance voted against it. Gearing the tax and benefit system so that it does more to help the poor is exceedingly difficult, but it must be done, and it is our belief that many of those who are at least comfortable financially are prepared to forego tax cuts in order to see more help channelled to the poor.

Government does not have to be based on the assumption that no one remembers the poor. The Alliance has faced some political flak because of its willingness to vote against tax cuts, its determination not to pay mortgage tax relief on the highest rates of tax, and its ambitious plans to reform the tax and benefit system so that more help is concentrated on the poorest families. In our view it is no use pretending that huge tax rates on a few very rich people will solve the problem of poverty: even if such rates could be collected without driving entrepreneurs and investors out of the country, they simply would not produce enough money. A lot of people on incomes which are no more than comfortable have to be involved in lifting the burden on the very poorest if the problem is to be dealt with at all seriously.

The particular problem of poverty among pensioners has tended to be deferred in the endless national discussions about the future of the state earnings-related pensions scheme which, whatever its merits and significance, does nothing for current pensioners. We wish to see improvements in the basic benefits available to pensioners and we believe that a successful incomes policy could make it possible for pensioners once again to have their incomes raised in accordance with the rises in incomes of those in work.

It was a Liberal Minister, Lloyd George, who introduced the old-age pension, and it was a Liberal, William Beveridge (my predecessor as Liberal MP for Berwick-upon-Tweed) who devised the post-war attack on poverty. The Alliance is committed to continuing that tradition.

'Heal the sick' (Matthew 10.8)

The healing possibilities opened up by a National Health Service offered, when it was first created, the vision of a country in which most major illnesses were conquered and the problem of sickness became a declining one. God does have a way of presenting us with new challenges, and as medical skill has developed and lives have been lengthened, new medical needs have arisen. We now find that the potential demands of health care are limitless, and call for fresh radical consideration.

This does not lead the Alliance to believe in the substitution of private health care for the responsibilities of the Health Service – we believe that would be a tragic reversal of the achievement of making health care available free to all, an achievement which has already been eroded by high charges for such services as dentistry. It does, however, lead us to believe that we must use NHS resources more carefully, making the primary health-care team based around the family doctor the basis of a larger proportion of treatment. It leads us to want to extend care in the community and the work of voluntary organizations, and in particular to help those individual carers who look after the sick in their own homes. It means that we must face up to the difficult choices which have been avoided by the formula of clinical freedom – choices between expensive transplant and other operations which can prolong the life of a few, and less glamorous programmes which may ease the sufferings of larger numbers or prevent diseases from striking very many people.

Preventive medicine and education have, in our view, a particularly important part to play. It was public health measures and simple immunization which saved millions from the killer diseases which were so familiar to our grandparents; and if we could tackle smoking and alcohol abuse, the impact on health would be dramatic.

'There was no room for them in the inn' (Luke 2.7)
One of the strangest of ironies is that the inn in which no room could be found for Jesus' birth has become the only home for many thousands. Bed and breakfast accommodation, some of it of an appalling standard, is all that can be

found for thousands of homeless people in the cities. A few are abusing the system, but most are simply the victims of failure in housing policy. There are not enough homes where people need to be if they are to have any chance of getting work, and many of the homes we have are inadequate. Some of the housing built in very recent years is now unfit and was never suitable for family life or for the development of a feeling of community.

Housing policy has been beset by dogma. Conservatives have insisted that home ownership is the answer to almost all problems; they have therefore increased the subsidy it receives and wiped out virtually all subsidy to rented housing, bringing a halt to local authority building. Labour has insisted that council housing should be the predominant solution, and Labour authorities have spawned vast, soulless, centrally administered housing estates and multi-storey blocks, in some of which no tenant wants to live. Some Labour authorities have tried to exclude any departure at all from the town hall monopoly in rented housing, even by the voluntary housing associations: the Liverpool Labour party contended that 'it is the local authority who must satisfy the needs of the working class . . . Working-class organization in this city lies in the Labour Party and the unions, not in housing associations'.

In reality, housing problems cannot be solved without a mix of systems and a diversity of providers. Buying will be the answer for some people, but not for others. Council housing is essential to meet some needs, but there should be a choice of alternatives. Different types of area – urban and rural, for example – face different kinds of housing problem. The Alliance, therefore, particularly when it has local political power, promotes imaginative and diversified housing policy, creating opportunities both for purchase and renting. We support the right to buy, but we do not want it to leave some areas with too little rented housing. We encourage partnership between local authority, private and voluntary sectors. We are attacked because we refuse to take up either of the dogmatic positions which we believe have made it so much more difficult to tackle the problem of homelessness. The problem must be solved, and dogma has not solved it.

God's earth

The Christian holds that we are but stewards of this earth, which we have on trust from God. It follows that we must care for it not merely for the present but also for the future. That is a long-standing emphasis of Liberal thinking which has been brought into the attitudes of the Alliance. We believe that all policies should be examined from an environmental and ecological standpoint, and we have been critical of those aspects of industrial, energy and agricultural policy which have lacked that perspective.

We have been particularly concerned about the development of nuclear power in the absence of proven safety standards and without solutions to the serious long-term problems presented by nuclear waste. Even those among the Social Democrats who have not shared the general opposition of most Liberals to the nuclear power programme have agreed with us that the present plans for PWR stations should not go ahead, and that a major safety and economic assessment is needed.

We believe that Britain can be much more energy-efficient and can make good use of its fossil fuels as well as developing new energy sources such as tidal power. It is not merely in the energy field but throughout industry that we should be seeking to minimize pollution and safeguard the environment.

The urban environment is one of which man has been particularly careless, and we believe that the desolation which has afflicted parts of many of our cities has contributed to the feeling of alienation which many people have. The dispersal of young families to modern but remote outer estates has combined with the decay of central areas to create a spiral of decline. We wish to reverse it, and make city centres attractive places in which to live and work for a wide range of people engaged in a wide range of economic activity, including the many kinds of small business which redevelopment has tended to displace.

Rural areas are also facing decline, and we wish to support those agencies which are seeking to sustain jobs and services in the countryside. The welfare of agriculture is crucial to the countryside, and will need much more sensitive and far-sighted attention than it has had in recent years. The urge to 'produce, produce' has given way to cuts in the face of European surpluses, and there are real dangers that the basic rural economy in many areas could be shattered. At the same time the loss of village schools, rural transport and other services threatens to make the country-side a home only for the rich and for those who have nowhere else to go. The maintenance of the rural environment depends on a healthy rural economy, which must in turn have regard to the future of the land on which it depends.

'Who is my neighbour?' (Luke 10.29)
Long before modern communications made it obvious that citizens of distant lands were now our neighbours, Liberals viewed the plight of oppressed people abroad as something which should actively concern them. Gladstone believed that atrocities in Bulgaria were in no way diminished by distance, and he railed against 'the negation of God erected into a system of government' in Naples. We have never accepted that foreign policy can or should be conceived purely in terms of Britain's interests, narrowly conceived, and it has therefore been a matter of explicit disagreement between ourselves and traditional Conservatives that we believe that morality is relevant to foreign policy.

In our own day our attitude has been illustrated by our long involvement in the discrediting of apartheid and our support for policies designed to force change in South Africa. Alliance concern for human rights extends to wherever they are taken away: we are not impressed when the left find only right-wing régimes to be in default on human rights, and when Conservatives criticize only the totalitarianism of the left. We are as concerned about the jailed dissident in Russia and the Soviet Jew who cannot leave for Israel as we are about the victims of military dictatorships in South America; we campaign when human rights are threatened anywhere in the world, whether or not the country concerned is regarded as 'friendly' to us. Human rights must be a key consideration in foreign policy.

But 'my neighbour' is also the starving victim of famine, the hungry child in a teeming third-world city, and the peasant farmer who cannot finance next year's seed out of rock-bottom prices. The people of Britain often seem more aware of their neighbours' needs than do governments — that became abundantly clear with the outpouring of generosity that marked the Live Aid appeal. The present government has greatly reduced the proportion of our national product devoted to development aid, which is far below the UN target figure of 0.7 per cent, while much smaller Scandinavian countries exceed that percentage and give more in real terms, direct to UN agencies, than we do. Any Christian in government ought surely to resolve, as the Alliance does, greatly to improve these figures. But we must improve the quality as well as the quantity. If we merely offload our own surpluses we may prevent countries from developing the means to feed their own people. If we do not assess the environmental impact of policies carefully, the long-term damage may outweigh the short-term good we do.

Moreover, we have to tackle the policies which are further impoverishing the poorest countries, from whom we in the rich countries collect more in debt interest than we give in aid. There will need to be policies designed to relieve these debt burdens, which were created at a time when oil prices made it convenient to the richer nations to push loans into the third world. We need to tackle the Common

Agricultural Policy of the European Community which, as well as generating unmanageable surpluses, is impoverishing primary producers in poor countries.

'Peace on earth' (Luke 2.14)
It must be the objective of Christians to maintain peace and to reject aggression as a means of resolving disputes. The reconciliation of defence policies with Christianity has occupied endless books, and the argument between those who believe that pacifism can be carried out as a policy of state and those who do not will go on until the end of time. For most Christians, however, defence policy is an area of difficult compromise made intensely more difficult by the appalling destructive power of nuclear weapons.

The Christian belief in our responsibilities towards our fellow beings must first lead us to want to seek ways of organizing relations between nations so as to minimize the risk of war. The Alliance has attached particular importance to the UN as a vital, although inevitably imperfect channel for argument and the resolution of disputes without recourse to war. We have sought to support and maintain a defensive alliance of democracies designed to deter and repel any attack on our freedom, but we have also sought to improve relations between East and West and encourage the dialogue which is needed to begin serious disarmament. Britain is not in a controlling or dominating position, although we possess nuclear weapons. We have a capacity to strengthen or destabilize the NATO alliance, and a very limited influence on the two superpowers.

In the Alliance we have concluded that Britain could do more to stimulate disarmament both by our readiness to see British nuclear weapons counted in the negotiations and by a refusal to escalate British nuclear weaponry as the Trident programme would do. We believe that it would be immoral and irresponsible to seek the security of NATO while refusing to accept the presence of US nuclear bases on our soil, as Labour proposes: we accept the full responsibilities of NATO membership. Although Liberals have long questioned the idea that Britain has an 'independent' nuclear deterrent, we accept that there are good grounds for Britain's retaining a nuclear component in its contribution to NATO, modernized as necessary, until it can be negotiated away in a global agreement which fully safeguards our security.

These are not easy decisions for any Christian, and although it is quite natural that politicians should challenge what they believe to be mistaken policies on issues as crucial as defence, I find it worrying that Conservatives in particular should be so dismissive of those who find the concept of nuclear retaliation morally repugnant. Those who accept the theory of deterrence, as I do and as the defence policy of the Alliance does, should not lightly dismiss the views of those who challenge it, and unilateralists should similarly not claim that they alone are concerned with peace or are exercising a moral choice.

Politics and conscience

The defence issue brings particularly into view the dilemmas of politics and conscience, yet it is an issue on which parties are obliged to come to collective views. There are other issues traditionally regarded as conscience issues and avoided by the parties, often because of the strong religious feelings they arouse. Governments duck for cover behind the private Member's bill procedure, and the parties usually make no attempt to have whipped votes. The present government came badly unstuck when it ignored the strength of feeling on the issue of Sunday trading, and was defeated when it attempted to secure a whipped vote on the subject.

Its term of office has also been beset by the issues of abortion and embryo experiments, in the face of a parliamentary majority willing to vote for some greater measure of protection for the human embryo. Those of us who have fought for this protection have been encouraged by the additional support we have now gained from a new generation of committed Christians among Alliance MPs. These issues still divide Christians, although it is my conviction that a growing proportion of Christians outside the Catholic Church, which has taken such a firm stand on life issues, now recognize that these are fundamental moral questions. It is clear that no attempt to turn them into party issues will succeed.

When it comes to the everyday decisions and choices of politics, conscience does not cease to be relevant, but what passes for conscience can sometimes be no more than self-indulgence. It is one thing to fight for a cause, and to refuse to vote for something which is morally unacceptable. It is quite another to insist on voting for one's own favoured project when the government of which one is part clearly cannot afford to satisfy everybody's plans, and difficult choices have had to be made. Nor can a politician deploy his conscience like a word-processor, sifting every word and nuance in every motion or bill that comes up for decision and insisting that nothing impairs his ideological purity. But the Christian who ceases to apply a moral and gospel-based yardstick to his political judgements is failing to 'take up his cross daily' so as to follow the Master, as he is commanded in Luke 9.23.

Belief and life

Christian belief makes great claims upon those who subscribe to it, in whatever walk of life they find themselves. Quite apart from the influence it has on an individual's political choices, it makes a particular call on him or her to show integrity, humility and responsibility for others.

Christians will find those qualities in some of those who do not share the same faith. The presence of other faiths and of those who hold no religious faith is itself relevant to the extent to which explicitly Christian values can govern our society, but we are not at the point where Christian values have to become the standards merely of a separated minority, wholly at odds with those who govern. There is sufficiently widespread acceptance of Christianity itself and of the quality of its values, many of which are shared by other religious groups, for it to be part of the standard against which our laws and administration should be judged.

My own belief is that the objectives and characteristics of Liberalism and of the Alliance provide the most promising opportunity available to pursue those values in the political sphere, and I hope that many more Christian believers will add their strength to the large number who have already made the Alliance the means of expressing their religious faith in the political world.

[1] Stafford Cripps, *Can Socialism come by Constitutional Methods?* (1935).
[2] G. D. H. Cole, *A Plan for Britain* (1933).